Yours truly,
Francis S. Smith.

PETERSON & BROTHERS

THE YOUNG MAGDALEN;

AND

OTHER POEMS.

BY

FRANCIS S. SMITH.

OF THE "NEW YORK WEEKLY," AND AUTHOR OF "MAGGIE, THE CHARITY CHILD" "EVELEEN WILSON," "BERTHA, THE SEWING-MACHINE GIRL," ETC.

WITH A PORTRAIT OF THE AUTHOR.

PHILADELPHIA:
T. B. PETERSON & BROTHERS;
306 CHESTNUT STREET.

Printed by King & Baird,
Printers and Stereotypers,
607 Sansom Street.

CONTENTS.

POEMS OF RELIGIOUS THOUGHT.

POEMS OF TRAGEDY.

THE YOUNG MAGDALEN.

THE YOUNG MAGDALEN.

A FISHERMAN'S hut stood all alone
  Down by the sobbing sea,
And there all day the fisherman toil'd
  And whistled merrily,
For his heart was as light and free from care
  As a human heart can be.
He had a tidy, good old wife—
He loved her as dearly as his life.
He had a daughter fair, and she
Was brave and pure as she could be—
As bright and pure as the sobbing sea,
With a face as open and soul as free.

"I wonder much," quoth the fisherman,
  As he stood by the sobbing sea,
"How folks can hear a sigh or a sob
  In the breakers rolling free.
I've listen'd to them for many a year,
  And 'tis music sweet to me—
'Tis pure as the bright sky overhead—
By it I earn my daily bread—
It has made of my cabin a charmèd spot—
I have braved its storms—they have harm'd me not—
And there's not on all the earth, to me,
A sight so grand as the boundless sea,
With its snow-capp'd billows rolling free."

One day a foreign ship was wreck'd
Upon the sobbing sea,
And her unlucky captain—a youth of high degree—
Found in the fisher's cabin sweet hospitality—
'Twere better he had found a grave
Beneath the sobbing sea.
Standing upon the ocean's verge,
Regardless of the seething surge,
The fisher girl his lithe form saw
Fighting the sea to reach the shore.
Fearless the generous ocean child
Stepp'd forth into the breakers wild,
And, whispering an earnest prayer,
She reach'd and grasp'd his long, dark hair,
Just as the struggle he gave o'er,
And brought him senseless to the shore.

Ah, me, it was an anxious night
Beside the sobbing sea,
When in the fisher's cot a group
Stood watching tearfully,
Much dreading that the sailor's soul
Had found eternity.
But soon their doubts were set at rest—
A wave of life swept o'er his breast;
And then his dark eyes, soft and mild,
Unclosed, and then he sigh'd and smiled,
And fix'd a look of glad surprise
Upon the fisher-girl, whose eyes
In sad confusion sought the floor,
The while a pang ne'er felt before—
A deep, strange, sweet, delicious pain,
Absorbing soul, and heart, and brain—

Caused her to tremble, blush and sigh,
And weep sweet tears, she knew not why.

There's something in the very air
  That fans the sobbing sea,
Which causes Love to grow apace
  And ripen rapidly,
And fill his youthful votaries
  With bliss and ecstasy.
The great, broad ocean unconfined—
The free, uncurb'd, resistless wind—
The billows in their wayward course—
All type Love's soul-absorbing force.
And so it happen'd that the youth,
Who knew not faith, who knew not truth,
Found favor in the maiden's eyes.
It was not prudent—'twas not wise—
But when was ever wisdom known
To rule where Love had fix'd his throne?
Her lover, with consummate art,
Ensnared the fisher-girl's pure heart.
She thought him noble, brave and true—
She worshipp'd as few maidens do—
No word she to her parents said,
But trusted him and with him fled—
Better had she been stricken dead.

And now the agèd couple stand
  Beside the sobbing sea,
And the great waves roll upon the shore
  In dread monotony—
And in its voice so sweet before
  They hear no melody.

It comes to their ears with a mournful sound,
Each plash is a pang each breaker a wound,
It sounds like the wail of a spirit lost
On a phantom vessel tempest tost.
And the foam of the waves which lave their feet
Reminds them of a winding sheet.
Oh, the waves they once loved so much to see
Are sobbing now in reality.

Months roll'd away, and to that cot
  Near by the sobbing sea
Came to the stricken agèd ones
  The anniversary
Of their lost darling's sudden flight
  To guilt and ignominy.
It was a black, tempestuous night
Without a single star to light,
The hapless mariner scudding by,
Tost on the dark waves mountain high,
The storm-fiend howl'd till all the air
Seem'd filled with shrieks of wild despair.
While rattling rain and lightning flash
Were mingled with the thunder crash,
And, all in all, it seem'd such weather
As heaven and earth might bring together.

That night of elemental war
  Down by the sobbing sea
The fisher and his good old wife
  In sweet humility
Were reading in the sacred book
  A touching history.
It was the case of one who fell
Like their poor lost one, little Nell—

And who frown'd on and threaten'd too,
With all her sin to Jesus flew—
Jesus, who shielded her from harm,
And quieted her great alarm—
And with compassion welling o'er,
Said, mildly, "Go and sin no more."

The agèd couple pray'd that night
  Down by the sobbing sea
That Christ would comfort their poor lamb
  Wherever she might be,
And save her from the deeper depths
  Of sin and misery.
And as they raised their tearful eyes,
A crash, that seem'd to rend the skies,
Broke on their ears—and with a roar
The tempest from its hinges tore
The frail, worm-eaten cabin door.
And there amid the tempest wild
Stood one who look'd like their lost child,
Bathed in the lurid lightning's glare,
With wild eyes and dishevell'd hair,
Her garments dripping with the rain,
Her ashy face convulsed by pain,
It was not strange the agèd pair
Thought poor lost Nelly's ghost stood there.

But soon a cry, sharp, shrill and long,
  Down by the sobbing sea,
Awaken'd in those agèd hearts
  A thrill of ecstasy.
"It is no ghost!" the fisher cried,
  "'Tis she, old wife! 'Tis she!"

Another instant and that form,
Fainting beneath the raging storm,
Was wildly caught and madly press'd
Close to a loving mother's breast.
"Look up, my darling! Let me view
Once more those eyes so bonny blue,
And let me hear you speak again,
'Twill still my doubts and ease the pain
Which long has linger'd in my heart!"
No word. The mother gave a start.
"Her lips are white and cold as death—
I feel no pulse—I taste no breath!
Quick, husband! place her on the bed!
Too late! Oh, God! my darling's dead!"
"No! See! She moves!" the fisher cried,
And then the blue eyes open'd wide—
And then a sigh burst from that breast,
Deceived and tortured by unrest—
And then a smile of calm delight
Broke o'er that face so ghastly white,
And then in accents sadly slow
The weary lost one murmur'd low:

"Home! Home! Sweet home! Hark, mother, hark!
   I hear the sobbing sea!
But oh, it had another sound
   In infancy to me!
For I was very happy then
   And from pollution free.
The dear old sea has alter'd not—
'Tis without blemish, speck or spot,
Its glad, free waters lave the shore—
It sings the song it sang of yore—

But now to me no joy it brings—
It sadly sobs—not gayly sings—
For I am alter'd—I have sinn'd—
And rolling sea and whistling wind
Will never sound the same to me,
For they are pure as pure can be."
The lost one paused and gasp'd for breath:
"Come closer, mother! This is death!"
The sweet smile never left her face—
One long-drawn sigh—one last embrace—
And on the loving mother's breast
The tortured bosom sank to rest.

And now there is a new-made grave
  Beside the sobbing sea,
And there the wild birds all the day
Make sweetest melody,
And the great ocean waves pour forth
  Their solemn monody.
The tortured bosom is at rest,
The sad soul once by sin oppress'd
Has flown to meet the gaze of One
Who pities all—who frowns on none—
Who felt the subtle tempter's skill,
And knows how weak is human will.
And can we doubt that He has press'd
The lost one to His loving breast,
And whisper'd sweetly, "Trembler, come,
Redeem'd, forgiven, to thy home!"

Sing, sweet birds, over Nelly's grave!
  Roll on, oh, sobbing sea!

For Death, the friend of tortured hearts,
  Has set the lost one free!
And what remains of her to-day
  Is pure as pure can be.

POEMS OF THE AFFECTIONS.

TO MY DAUGHTER, ON HER FIFTEENTH BIRTHDAY.

'TIS fifteen years ago to-day
Since Heaven sent to me
A winsome, blue-eyed baby-girl
As sweet as she could be.
And when I took her in my arms,
Her cherub face to view,
I felt a strange ecstatic joy
That thrill'd me through and through.

I watch'd my darling as she grew,
So artless, pure, and mild,
And sometimes sigh'd to think that she
Could not remain a child.
But now that fifteen sunny years
Have fled since she was born,
She seems as much a babe to *me*
As on her natal morn.

And thus I think 'twill ever be
As on the seasons roll—
The babe will still remain a babe
While tarries here my soul.

Yet, should she live, the time must come
When *she* will surely see
A woman in her looking-glass,
Whate'er *my* thoughts may be.

And when that time does come, I know
Her mirror will reveal
The face of one whose character
Is bright as polish'd steel.
She'll be as full of love and faith,
And pure as she is now,
And virtue's self will sit enthroned
Upon my darling's brow.

'Tis true she'll find life's pathway strewn
With thorns as well as flowers,
And she, when sorely pierced, may sigh
For childhood's happy hours.
But whether she be fill'd with joy,
Or 'neath the chastening rod,
She'll have the same dislike for wrong
The same sweet trust in God.

My darling, O my darling!
As time speeds on his way,
You'll find another love than mine,
To comfort you some day—
A deep and thrilling sentiment
Which you will think divine—
A love that may be more intense,
But not more true than mine.

'Tis right that you should make new friends,
 As through the world you glide—
I cannot hope to keep you, love,
 Forever at my side;
'Tis right that you should form new ties—
 'Tis nature's great behest—
Nor would I clip thy wings, sweet dove,
 To keep thee in my nest.

But this I know—whate'er your lot—
 Wherever you may rove—
You'll still possess, in all its depth,
 A father's holy love.
Whether beneath the parent wing,
 Or on life's troubled sea,
God bless my bonny, blue-eyed girl,
 Wherever she may be!

WE MUST LOVE SOMETHING.

WE must love something. Nature has decreed
  That human hearts should not all selfish be—
The gloomy wretch who feels no social need
  May o'er a brute display love's ecstasy.
The woman who hates man may love a flower,
  Or make an idol of a bright-wing'd bird.
The heart will long for something—love's great power,
  Since Adam's birth, the human heart hath stirr'd.

We must love something. Those who are deceived
  And feel the sting of falsehood and deceit,
Are apt to rail, because they are aggrieved,
  At every tie which makes existence sweet:
In vain they hide themselves from human ken,
  And o'er their bitter recollections brood—
Some flower, or bird, or tree they'll love again,
  E'en in their sombre, gloomy solitude.

We must love something—and if this be so,
  When we're deceived and wounded to the core,
Why not our sorrow to the light wind throw,
  And try that lottery, a heart, once more?
It is the best and noblest thing to love,
  If it be true and faithful to the end,
And in a second venture we may prove
  That full fruition will on faith attend.

WHEN FLOWERS THEIR INCENSE BREATHE AT EVEN.

WHEN flowers their incense breathe at even,
And sweetly soft the zephyrs sigh,
A voice speaks to my soul from heaven—
A voice of sweetest melody.
It whispers of those hours departed—
Those hours of love's sweet ecstasy—
That fled and left me broken-hearted,
And never can come back to me.

Oh, darling, as time hurries by,
To me thou seemest doubly dear;
And though fond memory wakes a sigh,
'Tis sweet to feel thy presence near.
I cannot, if I would, forget
Thy radiant smile, thy balmy breath—
I cling to them with fervor yet,
Though memory brings the sting of death.

Would I could cleave the ether blue,
And join thee in yon shining star,
How gladly would I fly to you
And leave this selfish world afar.
But all in vain my spirit yearns
To cleave the airy realms of space,
For until dust to dust returns
I cannot reach thy dwelling-place.

MEMORY.

OH, memory, in my day-dreams,
When a backward view I cast,
And in imagination taste
The pleasures of the past,
Though the present is all shadow,
And the past is in its grave,
Yet I would not, in my sorrow,
Steep my soul in Lethe's wave.

I have revell'd in Love's sunshine—
I have drank his dulcet tone—
I have felt the sting of coldness
In the heart I thought my own;
But as the bow of promise
Is born of clouds and rain,
So memories sweet will rise above
The memories of pain.

I have felt the death of passion
In the kiss of ecstasy—
I've clasp'd an idol to my breast
Which struggled to get free—
I have realized in anguish
What it is to love in vain,
And yet the memory of my bliss
Is greater than my pain.

Oh, glorious golden moments
  Of love, and faith, and trust,
I'll hug thee to my bosom
  Till dust returns to dust,
'Tis painful to relinquish
  What I deem'd reality,
But, oh! 'twere harder far to lose
  So sweet a memory.

In conning my past record,
  I find much that gives me pain,
And much that I would alter
  Could I live my life again;
But, oh! my glad soul revels in
  Those hours of ecstasy,
When Love seem'd mine and this bright world
  Was Paradise to me.

THE STEP-DAUGHTER.

SHE sits all alone in the church-yard,
In the depth of her sorrow and pride—
Her mother's a saint in heaven,
Her father is with his new bride.
No lowly-breathed word of endearment,
Or sweet consolation she hears,
And she rests her hot brow on the headstone
With an anguish too bitter for tears.

'Tis Sunday—the sweet birds are singing,
And bright flowers everywhere
Are lifting their heads in the sunshine,
And giving their breath to the air.
But the step-daughter sits in a stupor,
As though all her senses were numb,
And heeds not the sound of the church-bell
With its solemnly utter'd "Come! Come!"

And thus she sits hour by hour—
No rest, no refreshment, no sleep—
"Poor child!" cries a friend of her mother,
"I wish we could cause her to weep!
She sits here all day without speaking,
Till the gray of the twilight appears,
And the fire which burns in her bosom
Can only be quench'd by her tears."

Hark! The sound of the church organ rises
   And floats on the calm Sabbath air,
And a look of sad interest comes over
   The face of the mourner so fair.
And then as the grand choir follows,
   The eyes of the maiden grow dim,
And the bright tears gush forth, as she listens—
   'Tis her dead mother's favorite hymn.

Oh, wonderful power of music,
   Thou hast conquer'd the maiden's despair,
And I wish for her sake that her father
   And his newly-made wife had been there.
'Twould have seem'd that a sweet voice from heaven
   Their negligent ears had beguiled,
And have taught them to treat with more favor,
   That dead mother's sorrowing child.

HUMAN LOVE.

SEE yonder new-made grave,
   O'er which the willows wave—
No sound is heard there, save
   The wild bird's song.
Sweet flowers fresh and fair,
Arranged with nicest care,
Speak, in the fragrant air,
   Of friendship strong.

Those who revered the dead
Hang o'er his lowly bed,
And sympathetic shed,
  Uncheck'd, their tears.
Will flowers deck that mound—
Will loving friends stand 'round—
Will tears bedew that ground
  In coming years?

Or will the mourn'd-for dead,
When a few months have fled,
Sleep in his narrow bed,
  Forgotten quite?
And will the flowers fair,
Blooming so richly there,
Perish from want of care,
  Cut down by blight?

Alas, for human kind!
How seldom do we find,
E'en when in life, a mind
  To constant prove?
Then is it strange that we,
When death the soul sets free,
Should soon forgotten be?
  Such is man's love!

I'M SITTING IN THE TWILIGHT.

I'M sitting in the twilight,
   And I'm thinking of the past,
That was so full of fancy tints
   Too beautiful to last;
And as fond memory brings me
   Half pleasure and half pain,
There comes to me upon the air
   An old, familiar strain.

Oh, how it thrills my senses—
   That well-remember'd lay!
'Twas sung by one who long ago
   Pass'd from the earth away;
And as my glad ears drink it,
   In the holy hush of even,
It seems to me as though the sounds
   Were wafted here from heaven.

Sweet music! Holy music!
   Immortal as the soul!
How dead must be that human heart
   Which owns not thy control!
I have not heard that melody
   For many, many years,
And yet its magic influence
   Has melted me to tears.

Oh, mother! darling mother!
  It is thy old refrain
That in the solemn twilight hour
  Comes back to me again;
And while, entranced, I listen,
  My fancy is beguiled,
And thy sweet voice comes to my ear
  As when I was a child.

And may I not, dear mother,
  When my soul is call'd away,
Fly to thy side and greet thee
  In the realms of endless day?
And there in sweet reality,
  Be folded to thy breast,
And hear again the angel voice
  That once lull'd me to rest?

HOW LITTLE WE KNOW OF EACH OTHER.

HOW little we know of each other
  As we pass through the journey of life,
With its struggles, its fears, and temptations—
  Its heart-breaking cares and its strife.
We can only see things on the surface,
  For few people glory in sin,
And an unruffled face is no index
  To the tumult which rages within.

How little we know of each other!
The man who to day passes by,
Bless'd with fortune, and honor, and titles,
And holding his proud head so high,
May carry a dread secret with him
Which makes of his bosom a hell,
And he, sooner or later, a felon,
May writhe in a prisoner's cell.

How little we know of each other!
That woman of fashion who sneers
At the poor girl betray'd and abandon'd,
And left to her sighs and her tears,
May, ere the sun rises to-morrow,
Have the mask rudely torn from her face,
And sink from the height of her glory
To the dark shades of shame and disgrace.

How little we know of each other!
Of ourselves, too, how little we know!
We are all weak when under temptation,
All subject to error and woe.
Then let blessed charity rule us—
Let us put away envy and spite—
Or the skeleton grim in *our* closet
May some day be brought to the light.

KEEP YOUR HEART WARM.

KEEP your heart warm—be gentle and forbearing,
  Whatever trials may your path surround—
If slander follow you with tongue unsparing,
  Retaliation will not heal the wound.
Strike back with vigor if a foe assail you—
  Each man a right to self-protection hath—
But, the strife ended, hate will not avail you—
  "Let not the sun go down upon your wrath."

Keep your heart warm in spite of all mischances,
  And cherish love for all of human kind—
A morbid soul man's misery enhances—
  A loving spirit makes a happy mind.
In a true heart, crush'd by woe, love ever lingers,
  And feels more sympathy for others' ills,
As the sweet flower, press'd by careless fingers,
  Its odor rare more plenteously distills.

Keep your heart warm if you would taste true pleasure—
  Crush not the erring—strive their faults to cure—
He who his neighbors' acts would strictly measure,
  Should first take heed that he himself is pure.
And if you'd know the secret of contentment,
  Rebellious mortals, simple is the charm—
'Tis this: Lie down at night without resentment,
  Feeling no wish a soul on earth to harm.

THE CHIEF MOURNER.

'TWAS eve—a glorious eve!
The bright stars sparkled in the expanse above,
Like jewels in a kingly garb of blue,
And the round moon with its soft and holy light,
Look'd sadly down upon this giddy world.
The zephyr, wafted from the balmy south,
Kiss'd the sweet flowers and whisper'd to the leaves,
Whose emerald faces bow'd
In homage to their unseen king,
Who, gayly singing on his wanton way,
Call'd forth the ripples from the limpid lake
To join him in his gleeful happy song.
The whipporwill, sweet minstrel of the twilight gray,
Pour'd forth her piteous melancholy plaint,
And insect voices mingled with her note,
All joining in a vesper hymn
Which fell upon the holy hush of night
Like sweetest strains from a celestial choir.

Bathed in the moon's soft light the village churchyard lay,
Its marble tablets standing cold and still
Above the swelling mounds,
Fit emblems of the frigid, pulseless forms which lay beneath
In the calm, quiet sleep of silent death.
No more the slaves of avarice, pride, and black revenge—

No more the weary toilers up the hill of fame—
No more the zealous serfs of proud ambition,
But freed, forever freed, from all the passions wild
Which make this life a burden and a curse.

Beneath the drooping branches of a willow tree
There is a new-made grave:
No stone as yet uprears its marble front
To tell who sleeps below;
For but a few brief hours have pass'd
Since mourning friends stood round the solemn spot,
To see the sleeper placed within his narrow bed.
They saw him gently laid to rest, and then,
With eyelids wet, and heavy hearts departed
To eulogize his virtues—*and forget him.*

Not all, however, will so careless prove;
For 'mid his mourners one there was
Who did not leave the spot.
Motionless he stood till the sad rites were ended,
And then, when all were gone,
He stretch'd himself upon the piled-up earth,
And, with one mighty sigh of grief,
Gave up the life which now he did not value.
And there he lies prone on the damp, cold clay,
True to the last—chief mourner he of all.
And yet no stone will ever mark his grave,
For he is but a dog—a huge Newfoundland dog—
Who loved the dead with so intense a love
That the barbèd shaft which laid his master low
Pierced his great heart as well,
And so he fell a martyr to affection.
"All that a man hath wilt he give for his life."
Hero hath freely given his life for love!

SEND THE LITTLE ONES HAPPY TO BED.

SEND the little ones happy to bed,
  When closes the troublesome day;
Let no harsh invective be said,
  To ruffle their minds while they pray.
Sore trials and troubles full soon
  The sweet sleep of childhood will ban;
Then let them lie joyously down,
  And cherish bright dreams while they can.

Send the little ones happy to bed,
  Though they may be mischievous and wild—
Nature seldom bestows a wise head
  On a rosy-cheek'd, light-hearted child.
Then let their glad spirits have play,
  And brighter and stronger they'll grow,
Like a stream that runs free on its way,
  And suffers no check in its flow.

Send the little ones happy to bed,
  You know not what ill may be near;
Ere the morning your pets may be dead,
  Then vain the regret or the tear.
So let them lie down with delight,
  And fail not to give and to take
A kiss when they prattle "Good-night!"
  And a kiss in the morn when they wake.

WHEN FRIENDS PROVE FALSE.

WHEN friends prove false and joys depart,
  And life seems drear to thee;
When grief lies heavy on thy heart,
  Then fly, love, fly to me.
Be thou my only treasured guest,
Of all the world the dearest, best;
While pillow'd on this faithful breast,
  From pain thou shalt be free.

A selfish, sordid soul may know
  The blighting touch of care,
But hearts that feel love's genial glow,
  Are proof against despair.
So, when life's storms around us rise,
And fate her keenest arrow tries,
We'll gaze, love, in each other's eyes,
  And read our safety there.

Let courtiers fawn on royalty,
  Well pleased a look to get,
I'd rather win a smile from thee
  Than wear a coronet.
With thee life's darkest hour is bright,
Deprived of thee, life has no light;
My heart thy throne is day and night,
  My gems thine eyes, my pet.

KISS ME GOOD-NIGHT, DARLING.

THE clock has struck ten, Willie, dear, and you know
Papa has declared that at ten you must go.
Old folks are so queer! But perhaps *he* is right.
So kiss me good-night, darling! Kiss me good-night!

I declare 'tis eleven, and you are here still!
You know well enough *I'm* not keeping you, Will!
If you don't go at once, I must put out the light.
So kiss me good-night, darling! Kiss me good-night!

'Tis twelve o'clock, now, and papa's out of bed!
Don't you hear his gruff voice and quick step overhead!
Here's your hat! Go at once! Oh! I'm in such affright!
Quick! Kiss me good-night, darling! Kiss me good-night!

BE NOT UNKIND.

BE not unkind to the needy and lowly—
Charity's mission is lovely and holy—
Hard is the heart that feels not for its neighbor,
Doom'd by misfortune to groan and to labor.

Be not unkind to the agèd and weary—
Life at its close must be darksome and dreary—
Bear their complainings and foibles with meekness,
You may grow old and display the same weakness.

Be not unkind to the youthful offender—
He to the accents of love will surrender—
Force, for a time, his wild passions may fetter,
But, in the end, will it render him better?

No, his proud heart hates the strong chain that binds it,
And chafes, like a stream 'gainst the wall that confines it,
'Till, gathering strength in its spirit abhorrent,
It breaks its strong bonds and shoots forth in a torrent.

Be not unkind to a soul that comes near you—
Harshness and anger may cause one to fear you—
But what a recompense waiteth above you,
If you can teach the rebellious to love you.

HE'S TEN YEARS OLD TO-DAY.

LOOK at him as he bounds along!
  The red-cheek'd, bright-eyed boy!
His well-knit limbs so lithe and strong,
  His shout so full of joy!
School's not in yet—he's full of glee,
  And ripe for any play;
His little heart is full, for he
  Is ten years old to-day.

His roomy pockets plethoric
With top, and cord, and ball,
And rags, and stones, and bits of stick,
And other trifles small.
The hour is his, his mind is free,
So get not in his way—
Is he not rich? besides, you see,
He's ten years old to-day.

He is a prince among the boys
On this his natal morn;
Above them all you hear his voice,
Clear as a bugle-horn.
He laughs, he screams, he runs "like mad,"
No colt could wilder play—
But prythee do not scold the lad,
He's ten years old to-day.

O happy boy! so free from care,
How sad it is to know
That time will mark thy forehead fair
With trouble, toil, and woe!
But, haply, you're untrammell'd now,
So frolic while you may—
Though grief at last may shade thy brow
You're only ten to-day.

A WANDERER'S PRAYER.

FATHER in heaven, when my soul
Shall take its flight from earth,
Grant that my frame may perish on
The soil that gave it birth;
Grant that the friends who cherish'd me
In sunshine and in gloom,
Who sorrow'd and rejoiced with me,
May lay me in the tomb.

I know that when the spirit flies
Its prison-house of clay,
The wondrous structure, cold and dead,
Soon hastens to decay;
But though the pulseless, mouldering clod
No sense of joy may have,
My spirit will rejoice when friends
Assemble 'round my grave.

I wish no monumental pile
To mark the solemn spot,
No epitaph in fulsome style
To tell what I was not;
But I'd have those who knew me here,
As o'er my tomb they bend,
Say, with a feeling all sincere,
"He was a faithful friend!"

BE KIND TO YOUR MOTHER.

BE kind to your mother! Oh! be not ungrateful
When age dims her eye, or disease racks her frame;
No fault in mankind shows more glaring and hateful,
Than that which would lead us her foibles to blame.
She has borne with our follies in life's early stage,
And should we not, then, bear with hers in her age?

Be kind to your mother! Has she not stood near you
When loathsome disease caused all others to fly?
To comfort, to solace, to nurse, and to cheer you—
Yes, even if call'd on, to suffer and die?
Then in her decline you should never demur,
If you have to labor and suffer for her.

Be kind to your mother! Be duteous and grateful—
The heart's deepest rev'rence and love are her due;
And if of these natural claims you're neglectful,
Look not for respect from your children to you.
Each unfilial action against you is scored,
And when you grow old, you will reap your reward.

Be kind to your mother; for fast she is failing,
And soon she will sink 'neath the sad weight of years,
And all your regrets will then prove unavailing—
Your actions cannot be erased by your tears.
Then guard well your passions, be patient and mild—
'Tis the least that a mother expects from her child,

TO MY SISTER IN CALIFORNIA.

THOU art far away, my sister,
  And we miss thee when we meet
Together, as when thou wert here,
  To hold communion sweet;
We miss thee, and *another one*—
  Two seats are vacant now,
For one has had the seal of death
  Stamp'd on her angel brow.

Two months ago, two little months,
  The music of her voice
Would make the dullest eye light up,
  The saddest heart rejoice;
But now 'tis hush'd for aye in death,
  Her frame lies 'neath the sod,
And her sweet voice has join'd the choir
  Around the throne of God.

And our dear mother! oh! how well
  She bears the heavy blow:
A heavenly, calm serenity
  Seems mingled with her woe;
She merely says, "So pass away
  My children, one by one;
Still, I must humbly kiss the rod—
  Father, thy will be done!"

O darling sister! how my soul
  Is melted into tears,
As memory takes me back again
  To those thrice happy years
When *all* our flock were gather'd round
  Our happy, cheerful hearth,
And not a care was mingled with
  Our ever-rising mirth.

Now some are dead, and some, like you,
  Have wander'd far away,
And we have only memory's voice
  To cheer us, day by day;
Yet still we hug the darling hope—
  God grant it be not vain!
That we shall one day hail the stray'd
  Around our hearth again.

Oh! well do I remember now
  Your every word and look
When, bow'd in silent agony,
  Our last farewell we took;
My quivering lip and stammering tongue
  No solace could impart,
For oh! a fearful storm of grief
  Was swelling in my heart.

Then every loving word of thine,
  And every action kind,
With tenfold force came thronging back
  Upon my anguish'd mind.

As memory clings to joys that fly
  And leave the heart forlorn,
So those we love while at our side
  Seem dearer when they're gone.

Best, kindest sister, years may roll
  Ere we again can meet,
But thou art in my heart of hearts,
  While memory holds her seat!
Speed swiftly, time, increase thy pace
  Till the last hour has flown
That keeps my sister's anxious breast
  From throbbing 'gainst my own.

THE WILLOW.

I LOVE the lofty poplar
  And the tall, majestic pine,
I love the sturdy oak, round which
  The creeping ivies twine.
I love the generous trees that yield
  Kind nature's bounteous store,
But, though it has a mournful look,
  I love the willow more.

'Tis not because the cares of life
  Have steep'd my soul in woe
That I dearly love to gaze upon
  Its branches waving low.

No, 'tis not that; for while I gaze
   It calls up to my view
The sweetest, brightest, gayest hours
   My boyhood ever knew.

'Twas underneath a willow tree,
   Beside a running stream,
Where I in childhood, tired out,
   Had many a sweet day-dream
About dear Minnie Morrison,
   Who often play'd with me,
And whose bright face and sunny curls
   I even now can see.

O glorious Minnie Morrison!
   Full thirty years have fled
Since then, and you, perhaps, may now
   Be sleeping with the dead.
But if you still are on the earth,
   Wherever you may be,
I know that in your reveries
   You sometimes think of me.

O willow! dear old willow,
   Where are the friends who play'd
With me in happy childhood
   Beneath thy cooling shade?
Some dead, and some have wander'd,
   Some remember me no more,
But thou hast still the same kind look
   That greeted me of yore.

ALL BORN IN OCTOBER.

AFFECTIONATELY INSCRIBED TO F. S. STREET.

FATHER, mother, and children three,
All members of one family,
A curious thing indeed to see—
All born in sad October.

No birthday record do they need;
If they the year and day but heed,
The month is very plain indeed—
For each it is October.

All came when leaves were brown and sere,
And nature's face was dark and drear,
The saddest season of the year—
The month of brown October.

But may no envious autumn come
To cast a shadow on their home,
And may their lives be sunshine from
October to October.

Around the white throne may they stand,
A still united, happy band,
When they have reach'd the "better land,"
Where there is no October.

Father, mother, and children three,
All members of one family,
A curious thing indeed to see—
All born in sad October.

LET US CLING TO THOSE WHO LOVE US.

LET us cling to those who love us,
  And pity those who hate—
God's smile is still above us,
  Whatever our estate.
If loved ones fly before us,
  And those who hate betray,
God's mercy still is o'er us
  On sorrow's darkest day.
Then let's cling to those who love us,
  And pity those who hate—
God's smile is still above us,
  Whatever our estate.

The love that in an hour
  Will plume its wings and fly
Elsewhere to try its power,
  Is hardly worth a sigh.
The hate that would annoy us
  Is only worth a smile—
It never can destroy us,
  For Heaven rules the while.
Then let's cling to those who love us,
  And pity those who hate—
God's smile is still above us,
  Whatever our estate.

This life is but a bubble—
  'Tis ended in a day;
Then let us laugh at trouble,
  And drive our cares away.

The world has many a sorrow,
But many a pleasure, too;
If sad to-day, to-morrow
May bring great joy to you.
Then let's cling to those who love us,
And pity those who hate—
God's smile is still above us,
Whatever our estate.

COME TO ME, DARLING.

WHEN the red sun in the clear west is glowing,
And the soft wind from the sweet south is blowing
When the day's trials no longer are near me,
Come to me, darling, to soothe and to cheer me!

Thou art the sun that dispels my sad hours—
Sweeter thy breath than the odor of flowers—
Only thy smile can my sombre life brighten;
Come to me, darling, my sad heart to lighten.

You, when life's bitterness caused me to languish,
Rose like a star on the night of my anguish:
Nothing in life like thy dear presence blesses;
Come to me, darling, and meet my caresses.

Come joy or sorrow, I'll part from thee never—
Close to my bosom I'll press thee forever—
My heart is love's fountain laid open before thee;
Come to me, darling, and let it flow o'er thee.

POEMS OF SENTIMENT.

BEAUTY.

WHAT is it we call beauty?
  Who can the word explain?
The learned lexicographer
  Essays the task in vain.
There's beauty underneath the sea,
  On earth, and in the air,
And in the firmament above—
  There's beauty everywhere.

There's beauty in the flowers
  That decorate the sod,
And in the bright-wing'd birds that send
  Their glad songs up to God;
And in the lovely rainbow,
  And in the stars that shine,
And in the crystals and the gems
  Which glitter in the mine.

There's beauty in the murm'ring stream
  That seaward softly glides,
And in the herds who lave therein
  And quaff its cooling tides;
And in the graceful blue-wing'd fly
  That sports above the spray,
And in the nimble spotted trout
  Which claims him for its prey.

There's beauty in the human voice,
And in the human face,
And in the quick, elastic step,
And in the form of grace—
But these are finite beauties—
They are under time's control—
The only lasting beauty
Is the beauty of the soul.

The soul—the grand, mysterious soul—
Which cannot taste of death,
Because it is a part of God—
His breath—His mighty breath!
It bears the stamp of paradise!
It's home is in the sky!
It's beauty is eternal,
And all other beauties die!

There's not a pauper walks the earth
But carries in his soul
A spark of the Divinity
Which earth cannot control.
And in that spark a beauty dwells
Which cannot pass away—
A beauty which through sorrow's night
Shall find eternal day.

Remember, 'mid your pomp and show,
Ye proud ones of the earth,
The grandest of all beauty came
To light when man had birth.
There's not a wretch, however poor
Or faulty he may be,

But carries in his breast a spark
   Of the divinity.

Then aid your erring fellow-worm!
   Be not too prone to blame;
But strive to fan this spark divine
   Into a living flame!
There's not a soul so dark and vile
   But has some ray of good,
Which may be magnified if touch'd
   By glorious brotherhood.

LAUGHTER AND TEARS.

HOW sombre is that countenance
   Which laughter visits not!
'Tis like a gloomy, desert waste
   Without a pleasant spot.
It glares like some vile spectre
   On the sunny face of joy,
And haunts the mirthful, social group
   To poison and annoy.

The plainest face if wreathed in smiles
   Attractive will appear—
The laugh which wells up from the heart
   Is music to the ear.

That mirth should light the human face
Is part of Heaven's plan.
God has denied this boon to brutes—
No creature laughs but man.

And tears which from the bursting heart
Spring to the burning eyes,
Are, viewed by calm philosophy,
But blessings in disguise.
When the corroding ills of life
Cause every sense to ache,
If it were not for blessed tears
The tortured heart would break.

Then flow on gently, soothing tears!
Ring out, oh, joyous laughter!
We cannot live without ye here,
Whate'er our fate hereafter.
Smiles are the sunbeams of the soul,
When earthly cares oppress it,
And tears, when anguish comes, the dew
To nourish and refresh it,

Then let us laugh and weep by turns,
As fate may shape our hours,
For smiles and tears are to the soul
As sun and rain to flowers.
Laugh when you can—weep when you must—
And you will feel the better—
He makes a sad mistake indeed
Who nature strives to fetter.

SINNING AND SUFFERING.

WHEN you see an erring brother
   Cursed by some besetting sin,
Stifling every better feeling,
   Making hideous all within.
Pause before you frown upon him
   Or a word of censure say,
Recollect that it is written
   "Hard is the transgressor's way."

You would check your rising anger,
   And you would more patient be
With a heart that sins and suffers
   Could you read its history.
Could you know its fierce temptation
   When assail'd by passions strong,
You would pity the offender
   E'en while you condemn'd the wrong.

Heart enthrall'd by sin and sorrow,
   Sick with doubts and thrill'd by fears—
All thy transient, dear-bought pleasures
   Follow'd fast by bitter tears.
Trembling at the wild, weird fancies
   That encompass thee about,
With the dread forever present
   That "thy sins will find thee out."

No kind friend to soothe and cheer thee—
Loving few and trusting none—
Even in thy gayest hours
Conscience urging thee to run.
Feverish hope, unbless'd, delusive,
Flying ere 'tis half conceived,
Want's dread pangs, self-condemnation,
The cold world's frown and loved ones grieved.

When I see a heart thus writhing
In its sin-bought misery,
I deplore the faults that rule it,
But it moves my charity.
No wild, reckless child of passion
Can escape the chastening rod—
Life to such is only torture—
Man's less merciful than God.

OLD TOWSER.

COME here, old Towser—faithful still,
In clear or stormy weather—
And lay thy head upon my knee,
And let us chat together!
Lift up your honest eyes to mine
And list to what I'm saying!
Sit very still, old dog, for I
Am in no mood for playing.

You stole a bone the other day!
Oh! you were hungry, were you?
Well, don't repeat the act again
And this time I will spare you.
But how about the fight you had
With Uncle Billy's Rover?
I saw you when you ran at him
In yonder field of clover.

And then, how dared you tear the clothes
Hung up by Mrs. Hewitt?
Oh! you were playing then, were you,
And didn't mean to do it?
I fear you're growing naughty, dog—
Much trouble you have made me—
But, then, with all your faults, old friend,
You never have betray'd me.

And I can't say as much for some
Who boast of human learning,
And who have larger brains than thine
To aid their keen discerning—
Who hide their faces in a mask—
Who hate while they're beguiling—
Who fawn and flatter to deceive,
And murder while they're smiling.

And base ingratitude, old boy,
You ne'er was guilty of it—
Dog as you are, with all your faults,
You have a soul above it.
But I've known some of human kind
Who'd frown on those that bless'd them,

And pitilessly sting the hand
   That nourish'd and caress'd them.

Old dog, why do you shake your head,
   And squirm about, and wink so?
You think I'm slandering my race?
   I wish I too could think so.
I do not say that all are bad—
   Indeed, I think that few are—
But I reiterate that dogs
   To friendship always true are.

No doubt you're full of passions strong,
   And when temptation meets you,
You're like the stern self-righteous man
   Who villifies and beats you.
You'll stop to taste forbidden fruits,
   E'en though it brings disaster;
But, unlike man, you'll never prove
   A traitor to your master.

TWILIGHT MUSINGS.

'TWAS twilight—the bright-plumaged birds were at rest,
And the sun in his glory had sunk in the west,
All labor had ceased, and the whippoorwill's song
Like a dirge from the forest came wailing along.

A maiden sat watching with wondering eye
The many-hued cloudlets that skirted the sky,
Which seem'd, as they varied their colors, design'd
To furnish a type of the changeable mind.

As she gazed, twilight call'd forth the fair stars of even,
To light with their lustre the blue vault of heaven.
And soon like a host in their silvery sheen,
The pure lamps in ether were twinkling seen.

They spangled the heavens in dazzling array,
And night drove the sober-brow'd twilight away;
But still the young maiden in rapture gazed there,
"O night!" she exclaim'd, "thou art wondrously fair."

But e'en as she spoke, a low murmuring plaint
Came, mildly at first, as the sigh of a saint;
Then swiftly the storm-king arose on the air,
And left but one bright star to radiate there.

"Alas!" cried the maid, "'tis a picture of life!
How often is happiness turn'd into strife!
Bright prospects may light us awhile, but how soon
May frowning misfortune make night of our noon!

"Yet, though grief wring the bosom and tears dim the eye,
One bright star at least shall illumine life's sky;
For wretched indeed must that pilgrim be
Who cannot one pure ray of blessed hope see!"

SNOW FLAKES.

I AM looking from my window
  At the softly-falling snow,
And watching its still passage
  To the frozen earth below;
And I'm thinking of the thousands
  Who will hail it with delight,
And of the tens of thousands
  Whose comfort it will blight.

I mark the flakes descending—
  How grand to contemplate!
A myriad tiny feathers,
  Each distinctly separate!
I single from among them
  The largest I can see,
And in its devious windings
  I trace it easily.

And thus I learn, while musing,
  A lesson from the sky:
The flakes, like human beings,
  Are born to fall and die;
Each takes a common pathway
  As they to earth descend;
They have a common origin,
  And meet a common end.

The greatest, though conspicuous
While living, still must die,
And with the least in one low bed
At last must surely lie.
Be humble then, proud mortal,
Nor vaunt your high estate—
Death sees no difference between
The lowly and the great.

MAN'S INGRATITUDE.

WHEN at the close of sultry day
The wild-flowers on the plain,
All heated, cover'd o'er with dust
And perishing for rain,
Imbibe the gently falling dew
Which gems the emerald sod,
They meekly bow their pretty heads
In gratitude to God.

And so the bright-wing'd, joyous birds—
Those warblers of the wood—
Seem thankful for each blessing
That descends from the All-Good.
And ever in the early morn
Their cheerful notes they raise,
And send to Heaven their happy songs
Of gratitude and praise.

But man—vain, haughty, selfish man
Is never quite content,
He takes, without a thought of debt,
Each daily blessing sent.
And as the dew of mercy falls
To bless each fond desire,
Instead of bowing low his head
He raises it the higher.

Then pause, proud man, a moment,
And raise your eyes above,
And ask yourself what you have done
To merit God's great love.
Then walk abroad with Nature
When come your leisure hours,
And take a wholesome lesson from
The beauteous birds and flowers.

THE FIENDS OF DISCORD.

WHO are the fiends of discord?
Spleen, envy, malice, hate—
They lurk within the human heart
To poison man's estate.
With closest circumspection
They watch each little thing,
And when advantage offers
They are ready for a spring.

Oh, watch them well, ye thoughtless,
  Whene'er the heart is stirr'd—
Be careful of each motion,
  Each look, each thought, each word.
For, once aroused to action,
  You'll battle them in vain,
And lose, perhaps, that quiet
  You may never know again.

A harsh word when you're speeding
  To business away
May make some heart despondent
  Throughout the livelong day.
A frown—a thoughtless action—
  A gesture to annoy,
May wake the fiends of discord
  To banish every joy.

Be loving, kind and gentle
  As you journey on through life,
And shun the thorny pathway
  That leads to hate and strife.
Misfortune may o'ertake you
  But you can bear its smart,
If you keep the fiends of discord
  From warring in your heart.

THERE'S SOMETHING WORSE THAN DEATH.

OH, mourning husband, bending o'er
The ashes of thy wife,
Who, dying seem'd to take with her
A portion of thy life;
It was decreed that tears must flow
When first the world began,
But bear it like a Christian,
While you feed it as a man.

Bewail thy first-born's early flight
Thou broken-hearted mother;
And sister weep in anguish for
Thy darling baby brother;
And father, mourn, when thy dear son
Yields up his latest breath,
But in thy grief remember still
There's something worse than death.

It is to live to see the brand
Of sorrow and disgrace,
Mark'd by the ministers of sin
Upon the loved one's face.
Our idols may be safe to-day—
Their future who can tell?
Then let us meekly bow to Him
"Who doeth all things well."

TIME.

FATHER TIME is sweeping onward,
 Scythe and hour-glass in hand;
Nothing can obstruct his pathway,
 Nothing can his force withstand.
Now he blurs the cheek of beauty—
 Now he renders weak the strong—
And he cuts down all before him
 As he swiftly glides along.

And he seems a grim old tyrant,
 Stern-brow'd, merciless and cold,
Shaking mildew from his pinions
 On all things of human mold.
Making every pleasure short-lived,
 Touching love with his alloy,
Blasting with his sour visage
 Every bud of human joy.

Yet, methinks, if thoughtless mortals
 Would but read his visage right,
They would come to the conclusion
 That he is not ruled by spite.
True, he sides with Death at present,
 But he loves him none the more,
And in the far-distant future
 He will be Death's conqueror.

Then give Time the praise that's due him—
He his mission must fulfil,
And he'll use you very gently
If you do not treat him ill.
If you're free from dissipation,
And with vice no dealings have,
He will give you health and comfort
From the cradle to the grave.

BEWARE OF HIM.

BEWARE of the man with a countenance bland
And a tongue with a silvery tone,
Who freely his counsel will give you off hand,
As though your best good were his own.
Who though an acquaintance of only a day,
In his friendship excels any other,
And who in his zeal for your welfare will pray
While he sticks to you close as a brother.

He will enter your house with an elegant grace
And a countenance sweet and benign,
And you're almost inclined as you look in his face
To think him scarce less than divine.
He flatters each one of your home circle dear,
From the babe to the grandsire gray,
And little you dream when his praises you hear
That he's wondering how it will pay.

How harmless the snake, in your innocent eyes,
  As slowly his length he uncoils,
Till he strikes, and alas, to your utter surprise,
  You find yourself fast in his toils!
Then greatly you wonder while writhing with pain
  From the subtle destroyer's foul blow,
How a monster so poisonous, puerile and vain,
  Could have hoodwink'd and wounded you so.

Beware of sweet talkers unless you are sure
  That their language comes straight from the heart—
Praise from a true friend, who is artless and pure,
  Can have no appearance of art.
And better the tone of the blunt and the gruff
  Whom oft in life's journey we meet,
Than the musical, sweet, hypocritical stuff
  That comes forth in the tone of deceit.

STRUGGLING CUBA.

OH, spirits of the brave and just,
  Ye millions who have died
While fighting for sweet liberty
  'Gainst arrogance and pride,
If ye can aid a patriot band
  Determined to be free,
Then nerve those who are fighting now
  For Cuba's liberty.

On servile pens let fall thy power,
   And paralyze the school
That prates of Spain's supremacy,
   And advocates her rule.
Be with the patriots in this strife
   Till victory is won,
And war's dark clouds are chased away
   By liberty's bright sun.

And on the rulers of this land
   Thy subtle influence pour—
Let them remember how we strove
   To burst the chains we wore
When England held us in her grasp
   And treated us with scorn,
Till blood was shed at Lexington
   And liberty was born.

Now Cuba fights as once we fought,
   To free her native land,
And should not fair Columbia
   Extend a helping hand?
Down with ignoble selfishness!
   Speak boldly for the right!
At every pore brave Cuba bleeds,
   Oh, help her in the fight!

Oh, speak for her, Columbia!—
   That surely is not much—
Proclaim her sons belligerents,
   And deal with them as such.
Then will the monsters whose dark deeds
   Sathanus might appall,

Cry out with fear as they perceive
"The writing on the wall."

Then will the ruthless butchers feel
The vengeance of the brave—
The voice of doom will issue from
Each murder'd student's grave,
And soon demoralized and lost
The miscreants will flee,
And hurry back disgraced to Spain,
And Cuba will be free!

Oh, glorious hope! oh, blessed day!
Oh, solace for the brave!
A nation sworn to liberty!
A land without a slave!
Oh, God of battles speed the day
So glorious and so grand,
When one more hope shall animate
The slaves of every land.

FIGHT WHEN YOU MUST.

DEDICATED TO THE CUBAN ARMY.

PEACE! Sweet peace! Thou white-wing'd seraph,
We would ever have thee near,
For thou art the priest of order
To humanity most dear.

But when tyrants clothed with power
 Crush their fellow-worms to dust,
We must raise on high the motto—
 "Ye are wrong'd! Fight when ye must!"

Peace is lovely—peace is holy
 When it dwells 'neath freedom's light,
But when wrong uprears her standard
 Men must battle for the right.
Peace must fly and war must flourish
 When the vile would rule the just—
Strife, when waged for human progress,
 Virtue is—fight when you must.

Just resistance is a warrior
 Who goes forth with will uncurb'd
Conquering, that Peace may triumph
 And reign o'er us undisturb'd.
But for strife, throughout the ages
 Dark with ignorance and lust,
What would now be man's condition?
 Sad, indeed! Fight when ye must!

Peace is sweet, when back'd by Justice—
 Unjust war must bitter be—
Peace is bitter under tyrants—
 War is sweet for Liberty.
Then when men groan 'neath oppression,
 Battle must their wrongs adjust—
Peace is sweet when kept with honor—
 Not without—fight when ye must.

ODE TO POVERTY.

OH, Poverty, twin brother to Despair!
Thou source of woe! Thou summoner of care!
Dreadful task-master! author of misery!
What tongue can say one word in praise of thee?
Like a grim fiend of diabolic birth
You sit beside the honest toiler's hearth,
To mock him with your presence and to see
His wife's distress and his deep agony.

Ruthless you send your keen, envenom'd dart
With cruel aim into the proud man's heart—
High-toned, well-bred, retiring and genteel,
Too sensitive to beg, too virtuous to steal—
Reckless he hides away from human ken
And wrestles with you in his wretched den,
Till famish'd by your frame-destroying breath
He sinks at last and yields himself to death.

Your skull and cross-bones banner you unfurl
Before the weary, heart crush'd working girl.
You throw your icy fetters round her heart,
Unmindful of the bitter tears that start—
You see temptation near her and you cry:
"I have no mercy—you must sin or die!"
And should she follow guilty pleasure's train,
All hope is gone—she'll ne'er know peace again.

A few brief months of dissipation o'er,
A prey to thoughts she never knew before,
No power to stem sin's swiftly-rushing tide,
She ends her sad career by suicide.

Such work as this, oh, Poverty is thine,
Yet in thy presence man should not repine,
For sometimes (all with Shakspeare must agree)
"Sweet are the uses of adversity."

And ere I send my tired muse away
I e'en for Poverty a good word will say:
There's many a genius, it must be confess'd,
Who at the start by Poverty was bless'd.
Who would have idled had he been born rich,
Wasted his means and perish'd in a ditch,
But who, when want aroused ambition's flame,
Strain'd every nerve to capture wealth and fame,
And who, while struggling for the foremost place,
Developed some new fact to bless his race.

Many rich blessings that we daily meet,
Many inventions priceless and complete,
Both on the land and on the boundless sea,
Ne'er had existed but for Poverty.
And thus 'tis patent to the truly wise
That evils oft are blessings in disguise.

MY IDEAL DAY.

ON flies Time, while joy and sorrow
Greet each never-ending morrow—
Success and failure, hope and fear,
Clouds and sunshine mingle here.

Day breaks—we're aglow with pleasure—
Night comes—grief we cannot measure;
Now the banquet, now the grave,
Each crowds each like wave on wave.

Now my soul is sick with sadness—
Now my heart is full of gladness—
Now would I contented die—
Now cling to earth eternally.

Such are life's components real,
But I have a blest ideal.
I am dreaming of the dawning
Of a bright and glorious morning.

When all passions shall be ended,
And all faults shall be amended—
When man shall be pure indeed—
Love the law and truth the creed.

When the phantoms that pursue us,
Seeking ever to undo us,
Shall forever take their flight
To the realms of endless night.

When each gross and weak desire
Shall be purged by Heavenly fire—
When all evil thoughts will fly us,
And temptation cannot try us.

This the Heavenly sunburst beaming,
Touch'd with glory in my dreaming—
This my cherish'd ideal day,
When earth shall have pass'd away.

Oh, poor hearts with sorrow laden,
Only in the distant Aiden,
With a spirit newly born,
Shall ye find my ideal morn.

A FEW THOUGHTS.

I THINK a disposition that is happy and resign'd
Adds greatly to the comfort and the health of human kind.
I think a sour temper and a bosom fill'd with spite
Brings trouble, and puts every sign of happiness to flight.
I think no individual, however high his station,
E'er gain'd the praise of worthy men by vice and dissipation.
I think no dainty dandy, while for ladies favors sueing,
E'er added perfume to his breath by smoking or by chewing.

I think that wicked cunning never met with much success.
I think if swindlers suffer'd more their number would be
less.
I think if meddling gossips would cease to spy and talk,
That lawyers would be fewer and courts would have less
work.
I think that many doctors would better blacksmiths make.
I think that clerks who gamble have more than gold at
stake.
I think a man who marries, if he gets a proper mate,
Secures a fortune, though the bride may own no real
estate.
I think if certain folks would let some other folks alone,
They'd find more leisure to attend to business of their
own.
I think when stingy rich men chance from fortune's height
to tumble,
And meet with little sympathy, they have no right to
grumble.
I think that many ministers, renown'd for fluent speech,
Would more consistent be if they would practice what
they preach.
I think that true religion, when the tempter tries his art,
Throws a shield of triple power around the wavering
heart.
I think that every soul that sins will meet with suffering,
Whether that soul belongeth to a peasant or a king.
I think all grades of people, from the monarch to the
slave,
Are fashion'd from one common clay and equal in the
grave.

"WHATEVER IS, IS RIGHT."

DISTURB'D in mind, and rack'd by pain,
In solitude I sit,
A victim to the sombre thoughts
That through my fancy flit;
I'm thinking of the thousand ills
That human pleasures blight;
Yet through my musing runs this truth,
"Whatever *is*, is right."

I see the honest toiler steep'd
In poverty and woe,
While past him struts the guilty wretch,
Whose coffers overflow.
I see beneath religion cloak'd
Foul passions black as night;
Yet in my heart I feel the truth,
"Whatever *is*, is right."

I've seen the trembling culprit
A justice stand before,
And heard the doom which follow'd
An infringement of the law;
I knew the stern-brow'd magistrate
Was vile in Heaven's sight;
And yet I whisper'd to myself,
"Whatever *is*, is right."

The Great, All-wise, Omnipotent,
   Who sends the gentle dew
To bless and fructify the earth,
   Sends hail and tempest too.
Behind the lowering, angry clouds
   The sun is shining bright,
And we must take them in their turn—
   "Whatever *is*, is right."

I would not be misunderstood—
   I take no skeptic view,
I feel that I'm responsible
   For all which I may do.
But He who fashion'd me in love,
   Will judge me not in spite,
But pity while he punishes—
   "Whatever *is*, is right."

When passions slumbering in my soul,
   By fate to flame are fann'd,
He knows what my temptation is,
   How much I can withstand.
And if I fall while struggling,
   Or conquer in the fight,
He'll deal with me as I deserve—
   "Whatever *is*, is right."

The world is full of good and ill,
   And it is better so;
For if we never suffer'd pain,
   How could we pleasure know?
We should not prize the glorious sun
   If 'twere not for the night,

And love shows best opposed to hate—
"Whatever *is*, is right."

And if the All-wise wills that I
Should sorrow's chalice drain—
If he should change my hours of bliss
To misery and pain—
Nay, should he choose to plunge my soul
In realms of endless night,
I still should trust him, for I know
"Whatever *is*, is right."

Then let us take the good and ill,
Contented still to know
That greatest blessings often
From severest trials flow.
And if we sometimes faint and fall
Beneath temptation's might,
God's mercy still envelopes us—
'Whatever *is*, is right."

HAVE CHARITY.

THROUGH the great sin-blasted city
Toils a homeless little one,
Not a friend to soothe or pity,
Not a bed to lie upon;

Ragged, dirty, bruised, and bleeding,
   Subject still to kick and curse,
School'd in sin and sadly needing
   Aid from Christian tongue and purse.

But the rich and gay pass by her,
   Full of vanity and pride,
And a pittance they deny her,
   As they pull their skirts aside.
Then a sullen mood comes o'er her,
   Reckless she of woe or weal,
Death from hunger is before her—
   She must either starve or steal.

She *does* steal; and who can blame her?
   Hunger-pangs her vitals gnaw,
None endeavors to reclaim her
   And she violates the law.
Then the pamper'd child of fashion,
   Who refused to give relief,
Cries, with well-affected passion,
   "Out upon the little thief!"

Censors full of world-wise schooling,
   Cease to censure and deplore;
When the girl transgress'd man's ruling,
   She obeyed a higher law,
Take her place, feel her temptation—
   Starved, unhoused, no succor nigh—
And, though sure of reprobation,
   Ye would steal ere ye would die!

THE TWO SLEEPERS.

AN old man sat in his easy-chair,
Where he had sat before,
Day after day, at eventide,
For years at least a score.
The Bible open on his lap,
A smile upon his face—
And round his brow a halo shone,
Evolved by inward grace.

He heeded not the little one
Who sported round his knee,
And twitch'd the tassel of his gown,
And shouted out with glee
"Come, grandpa, put your book away—
'Tis nine o'clock you know,
And you must play awhile with me,
Before to bed you go.

"What! won't you play?" the child went on
With disappointed air;
"You said you would at nine o'clock—
Grandpa, that isn't fair!
But never mind—you're tired perhaps—
And I'm a saucy thing—
So sit you still, and I your pipe
Will from the mantel bring!"

And yet the good old man stirr'd not,
  Nor look'd he at the child,
Who laid her head upon his book,
  Gazed up at him and smiled;
And then she pouted pettishly,
  And then began to weep,
And then, tired out, her eyelids closed,
  And she fell fast asleep.

And thus they slumber'd tranquilly,
  The grandsire and the child;
And as they slept, it seem'd as if
  They on each other smiled.
But while the red-cheek'd joyous child
  The sleep of health was taking,
The old man was reposing in
  The sleep that knows no waking.

He had pass'd away e'en while he dwelt
  Upon the sacred story,
And left this sin-embitter'd life
  For one of brightest glory.
O picture rare! O lesson stern!
  For heedless man intended—
The wee child starting on the voyage
  The grandsire old had ended.

A WORD IN ANGER SPOKEN.

A WORD in anger spoken—
  How often does it prove
The cause of cold indifference
  In hearts whose rule is love!
How oft the swetest pleasures
  Humanity can know
Are by a harsh expression
  Turn'd into bitter woe!

A word in anger spoken—
  How many sighs, and tears,
And sleepless nights, and cheerless days,
  And weary, weary years,
Have been its mournful product,
  Though charity essay'd
To heal the deadly, festering wound
  Which thoughtless anger made!

A word in anger spoken—
  A blot upon life's page
Which oft will leave its impress
  From youth to latest age.
Man may forgive an insult;
  But still it bears its fruit,
For memory is a tyrant
  Whose rule is absolute.

A word in anger spoken
  Has oft engendered strife
Between the loving husband
  And the doting, trusting wife;
Has caused a barrier to rise
  Between the child and mother,
And led foul enmity to part
  The sister and the brother.

A word in anger spoken—
  If you have felt its blight,
Resolve henceforth to "know thyself,"
  And train thy spirit right.
Keep watch upon thy every thought,
  Thy every look and word,
And thou shalt live from sorrow free,
  As joyous as a bird.

A word in anger spoken—
  Oh! weigh the sentence well;
For it contains a lesson
  That words are vain to tell.
The human heart is faulty,
  And the wisest of us all
May drop a careless word in wrath,
  That we would fain recall.

THE POOR MAN'S SONG.

I LIVE in a garret, but what do I care?
I'm safer than some of my great neighbors are;
The loss of my wealth I'm not troubled about,
And my diet will certainly keep off the gout.
Then a truce to all grumbling, for happen what may,
While I've health, I'll be happy by night and by day,

There's old Mr. Graball, whose dwelling's hard by,
At the loss of a dollar is ready to cry;
And yet I'll be bound that the old fellow's dimes
Outnumber, by far, his quintillion of crimes.
Then a truce to all grumbling, the morsel I eat
Is honestly gotten, and wholesome, and sweet.

Then there's Mr. Freeliver, over the way,
Who groans with dyspepsia, day after day;
If Nature permitted, how quickly would he
Be willing to barter conditions with me?
Then a truce to all grumbling, for champagne, 'tis clear,
Is not so conducive to health as small-beer.

Give me but the power to labor, and then
As happy I'll be as the richest of men;
And the evils committed in grasping for gold
Can't trouble my conscience when I have grown old.
Then a truce to all grumbling, for happen what may,
While I've health, I'll be happy by night and by day.

THE BOUQUET-GIRL.

"BOUQUETS!" like a mourning spirit's wail
  Arose on the midnight air,
From the lips of a girl whose features pale
  Were mark'd by grief and care.
Her azure eyes were dim with tears,
  No purchaser she found;
And oh! it seem'd the woe of years
  Was in that plaintive sound.
Bouquets! bouquets! oh! pray do buy,
  At home there is no bread;
I hear my little brother's cry,
  And darling mother's dead!

"Bouquets!" and the poor child's tired feet
  Touch'd wearily the ground,
While the night wind through the lonely street
  Rush'd by with a moaning sound.
"Bouquets!" in a low, despairing tone,
  While onward still she crept,
And then between a sigh and moan
  She sought a seat and slept.
Bouquets! bouquets! oh! pray do buy,
  At home there is no bread;
I hear my little brother's cry,
  And darling mother's dead.

HEART-HUNGER.

'TIS sweet to feel in this sad world of change,
Where selfishness and pride so much abound,
That there is one, however wide we range,
To greet us lovingly when home is found.
One whom we know will faithful be till death,
Whose heart-throbs play in concert with our own,
Whose love will bless us till our latest breath,
To whose pure bosom falsehood is unknown.

The famish'd wretch who droops his head with shame
May be relieved by any passer-by;
The ardent youth who hungers after fame
Has always hope of feasting presently.
But, oh! to feel that we are all alone,
That love's sweet cup has vapor'd to the lees,
That there is no heart we can call our own—
This is a hunger nothing can appease.

To wander on without a ray of hope,
To find no respite even in our sleep,
Life's sun extinguish'd, in the dark to grope,
And hopeless through this weary world to creep;
No balm for us, no medicine can cure—
The ailing is beyond the reach of art—
All other hunger strong men may endure,
Except the weary, dreary hunger of the heart.

THE WOUND MAY BE HEALED, BUT THE SCAR WILL REMAIN.

OH, ye who from crime and pollution are free,
Watch well the temptations that throng around thee!
A character tarnish'd ne'er loses the stain—
The wound may be heal'd, but the scar will remain.

'Tis true that the vilest forgiveness may earn—
The sorrowing lost to the fold may return;
But sad recollection will bring with it pain—
The wound may be heal'd, but the scar will remain.

The misty bloom brush'd from the cheek of the plum
No more to its delicate surface can come;
And the pure heart polluted ne'er freshens again—
The wound may be heal'd, but the scar will remain.

The slave of vile appetites touch'd by remorse,
May weep o'er his follies and alter his course;
But still on life's Tablet his record is plain—
The wound may be heal'd, but the scar will remain.

Then shun ye the tempter, and seek ye the goal,
Which promises peace to the world-weary soul.
If ye sin ye will strive to forget it in vain—
The wound may be heal'd, but the scar will remain.

TO HATE.

THOU baleful, black-brow'd murderous thing!
Thou bane of human bliss!
Thou vampire fiend of sombre wing,
Whose loathsome, lep'rous kiss
Blisters the lip it meets, and turns
Life's sweets to bitterest gall,
And like a hungry fire burns
In souls that own thy thrall.

Thank God, I ne'er have known thee yet,
Vile monster that thou art!
Thou ne'er hast had and ne'er can get
A lodgment in my heart.
Though I were doom'd to feel the sting
Of enmity's foul blow,
I'd seek no shelter 'neath thy wing,
Thou minister of woe.

I can afford to pity thee,
And all whose guide thou art;
For no poor wretch from pain is free
While thou dost rule his heart.
I'd rather suffer from thy spite
Than own thee as my friend;
For love, thy master, will delight
When thou hast reach'd thine end.

THE WAIL OF THE BETRAYED.

COME, night, sad night, and let me hide
 My wretchedness in thee!
Nurse in thy gloom my woman's pride,
 My heart's deep agony!
Thy sombre shadows suit me well,
 My trouble and unrest
Are suited to thy darksome spell—
 'Tis night within my breast.

The flowers that bloom at early morn
 To some may beauteous be,
But those that ope at night's approach
 Are dearer far to me.
The first like sunshine friends may smile
 In fortune's happy light,
The latter will our griefs beguile
 In sorrow's gloomy night.

Though bright the glorious orb of day,
 It has no charm for me;
I would not have a single ray
 Shine on my misery.
Like the crush'd flower upon the plain,
 Dust-cover'd from the sight,
So would I hide my loathsome stain
 In everlasting night.

I love the dark-robed night, for she
   Shares all my bitter grief;
She has a sigh in every breeze,
   A tear on every leaf;
And while the moon looks sadly down,
   The stars shed, as they glow.
A ray of sorrowing light that seems
   Like sympathetic woe.

SPOIL THE ROD AND SPARE THE CHILD.

MEN and women, Shakspeare tells us,
   Are but children larger grown;
This is true as truth can make it—
   Few are fit to run alone.
Not an adult soul among us
   But some folly has beguiled;
Then when little ones are faulty,
   Spoil the rod and spare the child.

Anger only wakens anger—
   Love it is that rules the heart;
Force restrains, but does not conquer,
   Though the bitter tear may start.
If you'd reach an erring bosom,
   Trust to reason and be mild,
Give not way to brutal passion—
   Spoil the rod and spare the child.

If, with all his boasted knowledge,
  Man is changeable and weak,
Can he, with a show of reason,
  Perfectness in childhood seek?
Oh! then gently deal with children,
  If they wayward prove and wild,
Love will bring them to submission—
  Spoil the rod and spare the child.

Never yet did boy of spirit
  Feel the sharp lash to his gain;
If by love you cannot rule him
  You may lacerate in vain.
Glorious, bright-eyed romping childhood
  By each harsh blow is defiled;
Oh! then treat the darlings gently—
  Spoil the rod and spare the child.

THE DIFFERENCE.

A MAIDEN who spent the weary hours
  In going from house to house with flowers,
Stopp'd at a gorgeous mansion, where
She spread to view her bouquets rare.
Wan was her look and dim her eye,
And as she mark'd the passers-by,
Her youthful bosom seem'd to be
The dwelling-place of misery.

A lady from out the mansion came,
A richly-costumed, pompous dame,

Whose look of vain and haughty pride
The flower-vender terrified.
She view'd the poor girl's bright-hued store,
And turn'd the bouquets o'er and o'er,
Then ask'd the price, demurr'd, and then
In the rich mansion went again.
The maiden, footsore, sad, and weak,
Wiped off the tear that gemm'd her cheek,
And then again she pass'd along
Amid the city's giddy throng.
At length a bright-eyed working girl,
With ringing laugh and sunny curl,
Approach'd her, and in merry sport
A bunch of her sweet flowers bought.

But as the girl the money took,
The buyer mark'd her wretched look,
And kindly sought the cause to know
Why her young heart was touch'd with woe.
The girl replied, with tearful eyes,
"At home my aged mother lies;
She's ill, alone, and should be nursed,
But I must sell my flowers first."

The shop-girl paused and heaved a sigh,
A tear was in her clear blue eye;
She'd saved a sum to buy a shawl;
But "Here!" she cried, "I'll take them all!
My mother's dead, and doubtless she
Is looking now from heaven at me,
And she will smile—I know she will—
To see me hug her precepts still."

POEMS OF RELIGIOUS THOUGHT.

HEAVEN.

THE world is beautiful; but I
   Can see in all beneath the sky,
Proof that the Great Divinity
   Design'd that mortals,
To taste of perfect bliss, must fly
   To heaven's portals.

If not, why are our natures tried
By longings all unsatisfied?
Why do our towers, rear'd with pride,
   Totter and fall?
Why are the sweets on life's wayside
   Mingled with gall?

Music and discord mingle here—
The joyous laugh, the bitter tear,
The sunshine and the storm-cloud drear,
   All in an hour,
By turns will crush the heart or cheer—
   Such is earth's dower!

But there's a land beyond the sky
Where hope within us cannot die,
Where there is neither tear nor sigh,
   Nor strife, nor terror:
Where all is peace and harmony,
   Unmix'd with error.

There, bathed in light, we'll stand before
The One who human sorrows bore;
Who, houseless, famish'd, sick, and sore,
 Was yet man's friend;
And will be when this life is o'er,
 Time without end.

O glorious home! O mansion blest!
Thou recompense for life's unrest!
Close to the Saviour's bosom prest,
 How sweet to be
Loved, pitied, comforted, caress'd,
 Eternally!

FAITH.

O THOU! who holdest in Thy mighty grasp
The wide-spread waters of the boundless deep,
Whose blessed smile is in the sunshine seen,
Whose awful power awakes the fearful storm,
Who scattereth o'er the mantle of the night
The glittering gems that meet our upward gaze,
Whose voice comes to us in the zephyr's breath,
And greets us in the wild tornado's roar,
Whose glorious handiwork o'er all the earth is seen
In every plant that at thy bidding grows
To please the eye or furnish needful food—
In every bird that skims the ether blue,
To charm the ravish'd ear with songs of praise—

In every beast that roams the forest wild,
Or with meek patience toils for thankless man—
Thou Infinite! whose presence in all space is felt,
At once mysterious, awful, grand, sublime, and beautiful,
If I, a dying, worthless clod of earth,
Might dare to lift an humble prayer to Thee,
I'd ask that Thou wouldst teach me what I am,
And save me from the touch of vanity and pride,
Those twin fiends who, since the first angel fell,
Have lured weak, yielding man to misery and woe.
Save me, O Father! from the skeptic tempter's power,
Who with his specious reasoning would sap my faith—
And since I cannot Thy dread essence analyze,
And make Thee palpable to touch and sight,
Let me adore Thee as a little child,
Who cannot reason, but who yet can feel
Thy presence when he kneels to Thee in prayer.
I pray for faith, O Father! Faith to feel
That Thou art with me in this mortal strife—
Faith to believe that if misfortune lays
Her heavy hand on my devoted head,
'Tis done for some wise end known but to Thee—
Faith to believe if earthly friends desert,
If loved and trusted ones fly from my side,
That Thou wilt closer draw, and give that peace
Which none here can bestow nor take away—
Faith to perceive Thy hand in all that may befall,
And to exclaim in reverence and love,
"It is the Lord, and I am still content!"
O glorious faith! O sweet and heavenly trust!
Be with me to the end, and bear my soul,
In confidence and peace to its eternal home!

TO A SKULL IN OUR SANCTUM.

THOU loathsome, grinning, hideous thing,
So terrible to view—
Reminder of the dread, grim king!
Is't possible that you
Once talk'd, and sang, and laugh'd with glee,
As I do sometimes now,
With signs of pain and ecstacy
By turns upon thy brow?

How didst thou fall? What caused thy death?
Were thy loved kindred near
To see thee draw thy latest breath—
Thy dying words to hear?
Or didst thou perish far from home,
With not a fond one by,
To breathe above thy lonely tomb
A sympathetic sigh?

What were thy qualities? and what
Thy station in this life?
Didst dwell within an humble cot,
Far from the city's strife?
Or didst thou in the busy mart
Day after day appear,
Striving by every wile and art
To heap up treasure here?

Perchance thou wert a man of law,
And practiced at the bar;
Or else, perhaps, a man of war,
With many an ugly scar;
Or didst thou sail upon the deep
Thy livelihood to gain?
Or didst thou some vile hell-hole keep,
Thy base life to maintain?

Or didst thou strut thy weary hour
Upon the mimic stage?
Or didst thou lend thy mental power
To the historic page?
Or didst thou play a poet's part,
And in thy language pure
Speak hope to the despairing heart,
And comfort to the poor?

I cannot tell what thou *hast* been,
But I know what thou *art*—
A loathsome thing, whose hideous grin
Strikes terror to the heart.
I also know that when my soul
The better land flies to,
But a few months will onward roll
Ere I will look like you.

THE HUMAN HEART.

THOU knowest the heart, O Father!
And only Thou canst know
Its trials and temptations—
Its silent, secret woe.
No eye can scan its working,
Great spirit save Thine own!
Its innermost recesses
Are known to Thee alone!

Thou knowest the heart, O Father!
The lines of baleful sin
Will seldom mark the human face
E'en while it lurks within.
And there are those who walk the earth
From all suspicion free,
Who, when Thy jewels are made up,
Will have a part in Thee.

Thou knowest the heart, O Father!
Thou all its faults can see!
And Thou wilt read it truly,
And judge it tenderly;
And many a mourning sinner,
By man despised and bann'd,
May, when his deeds are reconned,
Be found at Thy right hand.

Thou knowest the heart, O Father!
   Thou King all kings above!
And we may safely trust Thee,
   For Thou art love—*all* love!
O glorious truth! O solace!
   How vain were human bliss,
If only man could judge us,
   And there were no world but this!

"GOD BLESS OUR HOME!"

"GOD bless our home!" is my orison tender,
   When the bright sun gilds the east with his splendor.
All through the darksome night while we were sleeping,
Angels a watch o'er our household were keeping.

"God bless our home!" As the bright day advances
Every new blessing our calm joy enhances.
Mercy and goodness still rise up before us—
Heaven's dear angels still spread their wings o'er us.

"God bless our home!" when approaches the even,
And the bright stars gem the blue vault of heaven;
By day and by night on our heads are descending
Rich tokens of grace from a love never-ending.

"God bless our home!" O Great Spirit supernal!
Keep alive in our bosoms a passion fraternal;
Let Thy love be the beacon to guard and to guide us,
And then only death can annoy or divide us.

A CHILD'S SONG OF PRAISE.

"Bless the Lord, O my soul! and forget not all his benefits."

AT morning and at eventide
  Father above, I call on Thee
To make me pure, to check my pride,
  And teach me sweet humility.
This is my duty, but I know
  It is not all my tongue should say;
From Thee all earthly blessings flow,
  And I should praise as well as pray.

Who shields me from the howling storm?
  Who watches me in slumber sweet?
Who gives me clothes to keep me warm?
  Who furnishes me with food to eat?
Who makes my limbs so lithe and free
  When with my little mates I play?
'Tis Thee, O gracious God! 'tis Thee
  And I must praise as well as pray.

For father kind and mother dear,
  And friends who are so true to me,
For all the good I see and hear,
  I am indebted, Lord, to Thee.
For brain to learn, and books to read,
  And grace to keep bad thoughts away;
For these, O Lord! I feel, indeed,
  That I should praise as well as pray.

And, gift all others prized above,
   Thy precious word, my hope and light,
Which fills my heart with sacred love,
   And keeps me in the path of right;
Which tells me of a Saviour dear
   Who watches o'er me night and day;
Oh! is it not, then, very clear
   That I should praise as well as pray.

Yes, while I live I'll praise the Lord,
   And daily strive in grace to grow;
Directed by His precious word,
   I'll walk where living waters flow.
Oh! praise the Lord, my soul, and raise
   And keep alive the sacred flame,
And all that is within me praise
   My gracious Maker's holy name.

THE BIBLE.

BOOK all other books excelling—
   Man's best earthly friend and guide,
Spring from whose pure source is welling
   Mercy in a crystal tide!
Heaven's sweet light shines all about thee,
   Making plain the way to go;
What were this sad world without thee
   But a vale of sin and woe?

God's own word! Life-giving treasure!
Solace when all others fly!
Who thy wondrous wealth can measure?
Who can set thy price too high?
Grief-dispeller—heart-consoler—
Faith-sustainer—sorrow's bane—
Death-destroyer—sin-controller—
Soul-enlivener—foe to pain!

Spirit-stirrer—vision-brightener—
Sin-expeller—sick soul's cure—
Strife-allayer—burden-lightener—
All-wise teacher—refuge sure!
Heavenly mentor—soul-wealth bringer—
Sinner's heart's ease—heaven's chart—
All in all—salvation-singer—
Balm to every broken heart!

Holy Book! How all should love it!
How its words refresh the soul!
Nothing earthly is above it—
'Tis God's light from pole to pole.
Beauties ever new discerning
As I con its pages o'er,
Let my soul have but one yearning—
How to prize and love it more!

PEACE, BE STILL!

LIKE a vast caldron seem'd the sea!
On sped the gallant bark!
Like a caged ocean bird set free
Upon the waters dark.
Shrieking the storm-fiend hurried by,
Speaking of woe and wreck;
But 'bove his voice arose the cry,
"We perish, Lord, awake!"

O wondrous change! O heavenly balm!
Borne on the storm-fill'd air,
A sweet, low voice fell like a charm
Upon each ravish'd ear.
It was the Master—"Peace, be still!"
He said, and the mad sea
At once, in answer to his will,
Was all tranquillity.

How sweet the thought when dangers crowd
Around us to appall,
That with firm trust we may aloud,
Upon the Saviour call!
How sweet the faith that makes all bright
And leads us gently home,
Where dangers can no more affright,
And sorrow cannot come.

SHALL WE KNOW THOSE WHO LOVE US?

SHALL we know those who love us,
  When this transient life is o'er
And we tread the Golden City
  That lies on the other shore?
When we shall reach the spirit-land,
  Will they to us appear
In all their old familiar guise—
  Just as we knew them here?

When we have cast this mortal off
  For immortality,
And the glad soul with eager flight,
  Speeds through the ether free,
Will it fly to its blissful home
  Without a taint of earth,
And find its friends assembled there
  To hail the spirit-birth?

Shall we forget our misdeeds
  And our miseries for aye,
And only pleasant memories come,
  Throughout the endless day?
And shall our love, refined and pure,
  Need no chastising rod,
But fill our souls with sweet content,
  And lead us up to God?

O radiant hope! O solace sweet!
How glorious to be
From all our earth-born phantasies
For evermore set free!
No longer passion's abject slaves,
All tribulation o'er—
How sweet to gain a refuge sure
Where grief can come no more!

LIFE AND DEATH.

HOW beautiful is life in its bright morning,
Ere the heart knoweth aught of care or woe,
Or the pure soul has felt the first sad warning
That sin envelopeth all things below!

How beautiful is life when, crown'd with roses,
Fond youth by turns rejoices, sighs, and loves,
Or in an ideal bower of bliss reposes,
Or through the sunny vales of fancy roves.

How beautiful is life, though proud ambition
Shuts out the light of childhood's happy years!
Man, striving hard to better his condition,
Forgets the while his misery and tears.

How beautiful is life, e'en when advances
Old age to bend the frame and dim the eye!
The tottering pilgrim backward ever glances,
And never, never is prepared to die.

But, oh! to me how vapid seems this yearning
   To cling to earth with all its woe and pain.
What is there here to quench this inward burning?
   What is there on this sordid earth to gain?

How beautiful is death! How calm and quiet
   The features are, fix'd in its sweet repose!
The pulseless heart—no sorrow now can try it—
   'Tis freed forever from all earthly woes.

How beautiful is death! That form so lately
   Rack'd by sharp pain and agonized by fear,
Now wears a look serenely grand and stately
   While lying silent on its sombre bier.

How beautiful is death! All strife is ended,
   Nor can ambition, pride, nor black despair,
Nor any other ill that life attended,
   Lay its rude, caustic, envious finger there.

O life and death! ye puzzles to vain mortals,
   And both so fair, view'd by philosophy,
Shall we, when past the gloomy grave's dark portals,
   Rend the thick veil that hides the mystery?

BE HUMBLE.

WHO glories in power? Who boasts of his might?
   Who worships his gold-heaps by day and by night?
Who makes only vice-gilded pleasure his aim?
Who strives only after the chaplet of fame?

Vain mortal! Thy power and might must decay,
Thy riches take wing and fly swiftly away!
Thy dearly-bought pleasure be follow'd by pain,
Thy wreath of renown prove unstable and vain!

What is this existence to which we all cling?
It passes away like a bird on the wing.
'Tis a breath, 'tis a vapor, 'tis a song, 'tis a sigh,
We weep, we rejoice, we grow weary, we die!

And this ends the story—the babe of to-day
Crowds out the grandsire who passes away;
And the babe in its turn hurries on to the goal,
Where death stands awaiting the flight of the soul.

Be humble, then, mortal, thou worm of the sod,
And bend thy proud knee in contrition to God,
Who only is mighty, who only can save,
And whose smile can light up e'en the gloom of the grave.

Be humble, and patient, and ready to go
Whenever thy mission is finish'd below;
Then rest thee contented, no terror can come
When God in his wisdom shall summon thee home.

ALONE AMONG THE SHADOWS.

I'M alone among the shadows,
And I'm waiting for the light,
To chase away the visions
Of the dreary, weary night.
Like a sightless child deserted
My uncertain way I grope—
I'm alone among the shadows,
But my soul is full of hope.

I'm alone among the shadows;
But my doubts and fears are past,
For I feel the sweet assurance
That the light will come at last.
A ray from hope's bright beacon
Comes through the gloom to me—
I'm alone among the shadows,
But my heart is light and free.

I'm alone among the shadows;
But I hear a sweet voice say,
"You would not prize the daylight
If it were always day."
And so I'll strive in earnest
To keep from error free,
And he who strengtheneth the weak
Will surely comfort me.

A WANDERER'S PRAYER.

FATHER in heaven, when my soul
Shall take its flight from earth,
Grant that my frame may perish on
The soil that gave it birth;
Grant that the friends who cherish'd me
In sunshine and in gloom,
Who sorrow'd and rejoiced with me,
May lay me in the tomb.

I know that when the spirit flies
Its prison-house of clay,
The wondrous structure, cold and dead,
Soon hastens to decay;
But though the pulseless, mould'ring clod
No sense of joy may have,
My spirit will rejoice when friends
Assemble 'round my grave.

I wish no monumental pile
To mark the solemn spot,
No epitaph in fulsome style
To tell what I was not;
But I'd have those who knew me here,
As o'er my tomb they bend,
Say, with a feeling all sincere,
"He was a faithful friend!"

H

WHAT IS LIFE?

TO eat, to drink, to strive for fame,
To lay up heaps of gold;
To pamper self; to toy with shame
From youth till we are old;
To tread the humdrum round of trade,
With disappointments rife;
Now fill'd with hope, and now dismay'd,
Oh! tell me, is this life?

Ah! no; 'tis but the grosser part—
A fraction of the whole;
The life which satisfies the heart
Is centred in the soul.
There lie the sanctities that chase
Away dark error's mist;
That fill us with an inward grace,
And fit us to exist.

Deep in the soul love rears his throne;
There truth and faith abide;
And where they rule, ill is unknown,
And life is glorified.
The outer world, though fair to see,
Is full of hate and strife;
And oh! how wretched must he be
Who has no inner life!

POEMS OF TRAGEDY.

A CHRISTMAS STORY.

'TWAS winter, and the frost king's breath
Made piercing cold the air,
And the rude north wind, fierce and strong,
Rushed through the forest bare,
Till e'en the gaunt and hungry wolf
Sought shelter in his lair.

Near the highway, and just within
The margin of a wood,
Lonely and drear, and frail with age,
A time-worn hovel stood;
And there a wretched couple dwelt—
Old John and Rachel Hood.

The keen blast whistled through the chinks,
And shook the crazy door,
And pierced the agèd pair as they
The embers shivr'd o'er,
And groan'd in bitterness of soul,
To hear the tempest roar.

At length the old man with a sigh
Upraised his hoary head,
And looking at the wrinkled dame,
In savage humor said,
"O wife! I wish with all my soul
That you and I were dead.

"This is a pretty Christmas day,
Old dame, for you and I;
All gloom, and poverty, and rags,
And abject misery!
'Twere better we were in our graves
And sleeping tranquilly.

"The pamper'd rich are feasting now
'Mid revelry and mirth,
And singing pretty madrigals
About the Saviour's birth.
Curse 'em! I wish the Holy Babe
Had never come on earth.

"How has His coming aided us?
What favor have we met?
Our only son a wanderer,
If he be living yet;
While we are old and poor, and scarce
A crust of bread can get.

"Religion is a humbug, dame;
'Tis only for the few
Who roll about in carriages,
And not for me and you.
I'd sell myself to Satan,
If he'd find me work to do!

"Hark! Listen, Rachel! What was that?
I heard it once before!
It sounds like some one knocking
For admittance at the door.
I heard it very plainly then,
Above the tempest's roar!"

The wrinkled dame rose from her seat
  And open'd wide the door,
And standing there, well wrapp'd in furs,
  A traveller they saw,
Whose face was bronzed, and who had lived
  Of years perhaps two score.

"A merry Christmas, friends!" he cried,
  As he survey'd the pair,
And then he wiped the frozen sleet
  From off his beard and hair,
And then he took a seat upon
  A rickety old chair.

The stranger look'd the cabin o'er,
  And then continued he,
"But you're *not* over merry here,
  To judge from what I see;
There are few bosoms that rejoice
  When pinch'd by poverty.

"But cheer up, friends; I have the means
  To make your old hearts light,
And I will pay you well for food
  And shelter for the night.
I'll make you to sing to-morrow morn
  If you but use me right."

And then the stranger merrily
  From his great pocket took
A purse of gold, and holding it
  Aloft, the metal shook;
The while the agèd couple stared
  With desp'rate, greedy look.

Uprose the old man quickly then,
  And eagerly he said,
"We've little food to offer you
  And but a sorry bed;
But what we have is freely yours,
  Though we should go unfed."

"Enough, enough!" the stranger cried.
  "If you give all your store,
You do the very best you can—
  The best could do no more—
So set before me what you have,
  And compliments give o'er."

The meal dispatch'd, the traveller spoke:
  "Remember what I've said,
You'll merry be to-morrow morn,
  Unless I'm with the dead;
And so a kind good-night, old friends;
  Come, show me to my bed!"

An hour pass'd on—the stranger slept—
  And to the agèd pair
It seem'd as though a thousand fiends
  Were shrieking in the air,
As they with greedy, savage eyes
  Did at each other stare.

At length the old man stealthily
  His trembling wife drew near,
And while his white hair rose on end,
  He whisper'd in her ear;
And then a groan escaped her,
  And she shook with guilty fear.

"Why should we hesitate," he said,
"To strike the fatal blow?
No soul on earth except ourselves
The truth will ever know;
I'll do it, though the deed should plunge
My soul in endless woe!"

Then crawling to the stranger's couch
He raised on high a knife,
And struck the blow which took away
The hapless victim's life—
Then clutch'd the gold and bore it to
His half-demented wife.

* * * * *

The wretched pair sat cowering there
Till rose the morning sun;
They could not sleep, for only half
Their dreadful task was done,
And they dared not by candle-light
Their victim look upon.

But now when rosy morning
Had banish'd storm and night,
They raised the floor and sought the corpse
To put it out of sight;
But, oh! their guilty souls were fill'd
With horror and affright.

With shaking limbs they raised the dead,
When suddenly the hair
Fell from the temples, and the dame
With fix'd and stony glare
Gazed on a curious mark, and scream'd,
"Look there, old man, look there!"

Transfix'd they stood in speechless awe,
 And motion had they none,
And freezingly through all their veins
 Did their weak life-tide run;
"Great God!" shriek'd out the murderer,
 "We've kill'd our only son!"

* * * * *

Oh! ye who scoff at God's decrees
 In unrepentant mood,
And sacrilegiously ignore
 A Saviour's precious blood,
Think of the fate which fell upon
 The dame and old John Hood.

"NOT NOW."

ON his bed of straw in a garret
 An agèd German lay,
And from a wound in his forehead
 His life was ebbing away.
Tired of this world's troubles,
 And crazed by the drunkard's bowl,
He had rashly sped the bullet
 Which was letting out his soul.

And as his senses wander'd
 He mutter'd o'er and o'er,

Of the dear old Fatherland he'd left
   Full thirty years before.
Something he said of Gretchen,
   Of the air and the bright sunshine,
And of his happy childhood
   In a cottage by the Rhine.

The doctor kindly tarried,
   Though he saw the end was near,
"Have you no friend?" he question'd,
   "No wife nor children dear,
For whom you'd leave a message
   Or some token ere you die?
Is there no one I can send for?"
   "*Not now,*" was the reply.

"They say that since you came here
   Full thirty years have flown,
And that you'd friends and money
   Ere misfortune struck you down—
Now can you think of no one
   On whom you can rely?
Not one of all your former friends?"
   "*Not now,*" was the reply.

"You murmur of your Fatherland,
   And of your parents mild,
And of the friends who greeted
   And caress'd you when a child—
Are they all dead? Is there not one
   To heave for you a sigh?
Not one, *e'en there,* to mourn your fate?"
   "*Not now,*" was the reply.

And now the dread Death Angel
   Shut out the light of day,
And with "not now" upon his lips
   The old man pass'd away.
Oh, who can tell while yet the dew
   Of death was on his brow,
How keen an agony was in
   That terrible "*not now?*"

LET ME NOT BE NEAR HIM WHEN HE DIES.

HIS face is fair—he wears a front undaunted—
   He walks among his fellow men erect—
He sweetly smiles as though no memory haunted
   His waking hours—he challenges respect.
His voice is low and sweet when his petition
   Arises from the altar to the skies—
His purest brethren envy his condition,
   But let me not be near him when he dies!

Ever on Sunday, at the sweet bell's calling,
   Will he devout and meek to church repair—
Shudd'ring, perhaps, to see some vile wretch crawling,
   Rum-crazed and ragged, from his fetid lair.
And as he listens to the earnest preacher
   The bright tears gather in his soft, black eyes,
And sympathy seems master of each feature—
   But let me not be near him when he dies!

He is my husband—we have lived together
In matrimonial gyves for twenty years—
I changed a girl's heart, lightsome as a feather,
For a long life of agony and tears.
The world knows not what I know—I've kept quiet
When I have heard him lauded to the skies,
All say he's great and good—I'll not deny it,
But let me not be near him when he dies!

I've watch'd him while he slept in silent terror,
And learn'd the secrets of his guilty soul—
Not one who walks the earth is free from error—
Not one can every little fault control—
But oh, the dark deeds mutter'd in his dreaming—
His fitful starts—his moans—his waking cries—
These are the products of his wicked scheming—
Oh, let me not be near him when he dies!

If in his sleep the deeds he has committed
Fills his lost soul with black remorse and fear,
If in his dreams he feels for Heaven unfitted
How will he act when stern-brow'd death draws near?
Oh, Heavenly Father, if in Thy discerning
The supplication which I make is wise,
Let me die first—for this favor I am yearning—
Oh, let me not be near him when he dies!

STARVATION.

AT twilight, in a tenement house,
In a small, unfurnish'd room,
A woman with her baby sat
Amid the gath'ring gloom.
The darkness seem'd to settle there
Like a funereal pall,
The while the flickering street lamps threw
Quaint shadows on the wall.

The wretched inmate glared around
Like a wild beast at bay,
As though she fear'd some monster claim'd
Her baby for its prey.
And then with all a mother's love
The infant she caress'd,
And drew it close, convulsively,
Up to her famish'd breast.

And as she hugg'd the little one,
A smother'd cry of woe
Broke from her lips the while she rock'd
Her body to and fro.
Then suddenly from her dark eyes
Uncheck'd the hot tears rain'd,
And in a voice of bitterness
The mother thus complain'd:

"Oh, baby, dear, in vain you toil,
   The wretched fount is dry—
The hunger-fiend has done his work
   At last, and we must die.
I've had advice enough, God knows,
   But words are only breath,
And pious talk will never stop
   The dread advance of death.

"They bring me tracts in plenty,
   And glibly talk to me
Of Him who died in torment
   On the cross at Calvary.
Whene'er they come to visit me
   The lesson they repeat,
But I think I'd learn it better
   If I had enough to eat.

"They say I have a sinful soul
   For which the Saviour bled,
But I've a mortal body too,
   And should not that be fed?
I do not scorn their teachings—
   I have tried in prayer to kneel—
But when the body is unfed
   The spirit will not feel.

"For food and a physician's aid
   In vain aloud I cry—
My darling babe is sinking fast,
   I cannot see him die!
He struggles at my bosom
   Till his little strength is spent,

And, oh, it breaks my heart to know
He finds no nourishment,

"Oh, wealthy mothers of the land,
Whose nurslings grow and thrive,
Give me a single loaf of bread
To keep my babe alive.
And when I see the tint of health
Upon his pale cheek start,
I'll read your tracts, and pray that God
Will purify my heart.

"But now throughout the livelong day,
The spectre of despair
Stands at my side and glares at me,
And I can say no prayer.
And would not you rebellious be
And full of wild unrest,
If the sweet babe you love so much
Were starving on your breast?

"Your prayer begins, '*Our* Father,'
So we must sisters be—
And should not then a sister feel
A sister's misery?
Give, give me food, ye proud ones,
And let it not be said
That one with store of gold refused
A dying sister bread.

"But all in vain I supplicate—
No succor will they yield,
And we, my babe, will shortly be
At rest in Potter's Field.

And oh, I wish the time had come,
For death I do not fear,
The life beyond must happier be
Than that we pass through here."

ALONE.

IN a poverty-stricken hovel
Stood a man in deep despair,
For his wife, his love, his darling,
Lay stark and silent there.
They had struggled on together—
Had pain and hunger known—
But he never thought of trouble
Till he stood on earth alone.

"Speak to me, Mary, darling!"
The wretched mourner said,
"My love, my life, my dear one!
It can't be that you're dead!
Your Dermott's heart is bursting
With this bitter, bitter pain!
Oh, open your eyes, *mavourneen*,
And speak to me once again!"

"She's dead enough, I warrant!"
A surly neighbor said,
"And in my candid thinking
It's better that she's dead.

You've ran yourself in debt, man,
  Since she's been lying ill,
And what you earn while working
  One mouth will scarcely fill."

"Oh, man!" cried the bereaved one,
  "Sure, you have never known
What 'tis in this cold, selfish world
  To feel yourself *alone!*
Alone! while the heart is aching,
  Through the dreary, weary night,
Alone! when the birds are singing
  And the sun is shining bright!

"You don't know what it is, man,
  When life you're passing through,
To feel that there's no heart on earth
  That beats with love for you.
No loving hand to minister
  When sickness brings you low—
No loving voice to cheer you
  In the midst of gloom and woe.

"'Tis true my only darling
  And myself had toil and care,
But still we did not murmur
  At our labor or our fare,
With words of love and comfort
  Our daily crust we shared,
And thank'd the Blessed Giver
  That *heart-hunger* we were spared.

"Believe me—oh, believe me—
That in this world so cold
'Tis better to be rich in love
Than rich in lands and gold.
If you've true love to comfort you
While on the hours fly,
You've that which all the wealth on earth
Can neither filch nor buy.

"Oh, Mary, Mary, darling!
I'll sit with you to-night,
And I'll fancy you are living
Till you're buried out of sight—
And my heart will still be with you
When you sleep beneath the sod,
And I'll see you in my dreaming
Till I'm call'd away to God."

"PLEASE BURY MY LITTLE DARLING."

["Please bury my little darling. I am driven by poverty and an intemperate husband to do that I would not do. I shall soon be with my child." It was the old, old story, pinned on the clothing of an infant found dead yesterday, and buried in the Potter's Field.—*New York Sun.*]

I AM weary, oh, how weary
Of the trials and the fears
That have haunted me like spectres
So many bitter years.
My eyes are sear'd with weeping
'Mid poverty and strife—
Please bury my little darling
For I have done with life.

In the silence of the midnight,
With my baby on my breast,
I've pray'd that God might summon us
To His eternal rest.
He has taken my sweet infant
And answer'd half my prayer,
Please bury my little darling
And I will join him there.

Is it strange that I should murmur,
And long so much to flee
Far from a rum-crazed husband
And abject poverty?
I am wild with this great torture,
And my head begins to swim,
Please bury my little darling
For I must go to him.

He cannot come to me—ah, no,
My babe has gone to rest—
His tiny hands are folded
Upon his little breast.
His soul is with the Saviour,
Who has borne it to the sky—
Please bury my little darling,
And now, cold world, good-by!

DEATH IN THE TOMB.

WHO knows him, officer? Has he no friend?
No one who'll shudder to think of his end?
No one to pray for him?
No one to say for him
One gentle word that no ear may offend?
Is there no tender heart,
Feeling a brother's part,
That his remains to the grave will attend?

You found him, did you, while walking your beat,
Stupid with liquor, stretch'd prone on the street?
In a cart placed him then,
Hitherward raced him then,
And in the court held him up on his feet,
While you the charge preferr'd,
Nothing of which he heard,
And his committal was render'd complete?

He was found dead, was he, after a spell—
Died all alone in this horrible cell—
No one to hear his cries,
No one to close his eyes,
Man, if you have a heart, say was it well?
How do you know 'twas drink
That caused his frame to sink?
Was it not something else? ah, who can tell?

Ah, poor unknown! while he lies in death here,
Somebody's waiting his footsteps to hear—
Sad wife and children may
Hope on from day to day,
That the dear light of their hearts may appear.
But they will look in vain
Ne'er will he come again
With his glad tones their sad bosoms to cheer.

THE DRUNKARD.

HOPELESSLY wandering through the cold street,
His clothes all in tatters, no shoes on his feet;
With countenance bloated, and rum-frenzied eye,
Tired of living, yet fearing to die,
How the crowd jeers as he shuffles along,
No look of pity or love in the throng;
How his heart burns as he looks on the scene,
Thinking of what *is* and what might have been!

Once he was youthful, light-hearted, and gay—
Life to him then seem'd a long summer's day;
Now he is penniless, friendless, and old,
And shakes like a reed in the pitiless cold.
Once he had energy, freedom from fear,
A bright beaming eye, and an intellect clear;
'Twas seldom that sorrow or trouble would come,
Till he gave himself up to the demon of rum.

Drink was the serpent that wrought his first pain,
And fix'd on his record unsullied, a stain;
Drink that he hail'd as a friend in his glee,
But oh! what a fiend did that friend prove to be!
Slowly, but surely, with devilish art,
It palsied his strong frame and ate out his heart,
And placed the dark brand of disgrace on his brow,
And made him that wreck of a man he is now.

O ye who are under the rum-demon's spell,
And pour down your throats his vile poison of hell!
Of his subtle arts I beseech you beware,
Ere you find yourselves wreck'd on the shoal of despair.
Ye may fight him a while, but believe me, at length
The strongest will fall and succumb to his strength;
If you court him at all, you will struggle in vain
To break the strong links of the rum-demon's chain.

THE DRUNKARD'S WIFE.

I AM dying, Willie, dying,
  Death's dew is on my brow;
Come closer—let me gaze on you,
  For you are sober now.
Your eyes beam kindly on me—
  Your voice is soft and low—
And your presence brings to light again
  The blessed long ago.

I'm thinking of the happy time
   Ere you and I were wed,
When daily blessings seem'd to fall
   Like incense on my head—
When great joy fill'd my bosom,
   And my step was light and free,
And you, a bright-eyed, fearless boy,
   Were all the world to me.

Oh, how I loved you, Willie!
   And I love you, darling, yet—
Your kindness in that golden time
   I never can forget.
And I do not mean to chide you,
   When a backward view I cast;
And shudder at the gulf between
   The present and the past.

Forgive me, Willie, darling,
   If my words have caused you pain—
I will not call up memories
   Of the long ago again.
But I must speak of the present,
   For I have that to say
Which I would have you think of,
   When I am snatch'd away.

Our little boy, oh, Willie,
   He is pure and sinless now—
There is no shade of crime or vice
   Upon his baby brow—
His heart is free from bitterness—
   His soul is pure as snow—

Oh, Willie, in the years to come
   See that you keep him so.

You have sworn upon the Bible
   That you ne'er again will taste
The poison that has ruin'd us
   And made our lives a waste.
If you keep that solemn covenant
   As long as life shall last,
Our boy is safe, and God will grant
   Forgiveness for the past.

Come closer to me, darling,
   Let me fold you to my breast,
Ere the shadows close around me
   And I sink to dreamless rest.
Oh, the weary, weary hours,
   And the bitter, bitter pain,
Are lifted from my bosom
   And all is peace again.

I am dying, Willie, dying,
   But for me all pain is o'er;
And I'll look for you, my darling,
   When I reach the golden shore.
God will'd that I should perish
   To save you and our boy,
And I go to seek His presence
   With an eager, eager joy.

LINES ON THE DEATH OF A YOUNG LADY WHO DIED ONLY FOUR WEEKS AFTER MARRIAGE.

PROUDLY stood they at the altar,
Loving friends on every side—
He a young and joyous bridegroom,
She a youthful, blushing bride.
Pure her soul as were the flowers
That enwreathed her virgin brow—
Pass'd she like a vision from us,
And she is an angel now.

Four short weeks a bride was Carrie,
Full of wedded happiness,
Then we laid her down to slumber
In her pure white bridal dress.
Brilliant was she in her beauty,
As she took her nuptial vow,
But she was too pure for earth-life,
And she is an angel now.

Jesus wept o'er the departed—
Even He felt mortal woe—
And when loved ones vanish from us,
Hearts *will* ache and tears will flow.
Weep then, friends, and stricken husband
But in meek submission bow
To the will of God—for, surely,
Carrie is an angel now.

THE TYRANT KING.

OH, I am a mighty monarch—
No mightier can be—
For tens of thousands yearly
Lay down their lives for me.
My subjects love me dearly,
With all my tyranny.

Among earth's mighty rulers
No rival do I own—
Beneath my vile exactions
My meek slaves daily groan,
And yet, 'mid feuds and factions,
I'm firm upon my throne.

No other heartless tyrant
Could foster hate and strife,
Without the greatest danger
Of forfeiting his life,
And yet, to fear a strangér,
I rove, with malice rife.

You'll wonder when I tell you
How reckless I can be—
What dark deeds I am doing
With all impunity—
What evil paths pursuing
While millions cling to me.

I urge, when wild with passion,
Weak man to kill his brother—
I foster bitterness and hate
Between the child and mother—
I cause the father's heart irate
Each spark of love to smother.

I touch, with smile seductive,
A matron pure and true,
And she for me will peril
Her soul and body, too—
That bosom render'd sterile,
Where truth and virtue grew.

Yea, she will shame the wild-cat
In her rage, at my behest,
And slay the babe who cowers
On her besotted breast,
And curse the wretched hours
In her frenzy and unrest.

I see a man respected—
A husband good and brave—
I throw my toils around him
And claim him for my slave.
He licks the hand that bound him,
And finds an early grave.

Or he may live to scoff at
And violate the law—
Perhaps to bathe, when madden'd,
His hands in human gore,
While fiends in Hades, gladden'd,
Will gloat his ruin o'er.

My loyal slaves are legion—
   They fill our social hells,
And groan their brief existence
   Away in prison cells.
In sinning, their persistence
   My wond'rous power tells.

For me men weep and travail
   In rags and wretchedness,
Without a ray of kindness
   Their tortured lives to bless,
And beg me in their blindness,
   To banish their distress.

A man will sell his daughter,
   Or his wedded wife for me—
The son betray his father
   To basest ignomy—
Then hug my shackles, rather
   Than be innocent and free.

There's not a crime prevailing
   That I do not incite—
They may be scored by millions
   Whose happiness I blight—
Indeed I've slain my billions
   Since first I saw the light.

And yet my timid vassals
   Are safe beneath my thumb—
If they complain, a visit
   From me will make them dumb.
You ask my name? What is it?
   My name, oh, man, is RUM!

WORLD-WEARY.

WEARY, weary, oh! how weary
  Is she of the cold world's strife!
Dreary, dreary, oh! how dreary
  Is the path of her sad life!
Grim the phantoms that pursue her
  Ever, ever, night and day!
Whispering dark words unto her,
  Chasing hope and faith away.

Not a trusted friend is near her,
  In the world she stands alone;
None to soothe her, none to cheer her,
  Wrong'd, uncared for, and unknown.
Gazes she upon the water,
  Dazed her brain and wild her eye,
Breathes the prayer her mother taught her,
  And then plunges in to die!

Rash the deed, but judge her kindly
  Ye who gaze on horrified!
Had she never loved so blindly,
  She would never thus have died.
Raise her form, all bruised and broken,
  Lay it gently 'neath the sod;
Let not one harsh word be spoken,
  Leave her failings all with God.

THE OUTCAST.

(AN "OW'RE TRUE TALE.")

A YOUTH sat weeping silently,
And on his woful face,
Once innocent, might now be seen
The shadow of disgrace.
He'd fallen from his high estate,
And sought for peace in vain.
"My reputation's gone!" he cried,
"I ne'er can smile again!"

But as he shed in bitterness
The penitential tear,
His friends approach'd, and soothing words
They whisper'd in his ear.
They bade him blot from memory's page
The past, and keep in view
The future only, that he might
Commence his life anew.

He did so, and a little while
His soul was pure and free
From evil thoughts, temptation's power,
And all unchastity.
But soon by guilty pleasure's shaft
Again his heart was riven;
Once more he fell, but by his friends
He was once more forgiven.

And there was one, through all his guilt,
   Forever at his side,
Who strove with more than human love
   His glaring faults to hide.
In every dark and stormy time
   A sister near him stood,
Beseeching him to shun the ill,
   And learn to choose the good.

A year roll'd by, and in that time,
   Lamentable to tell,
The victim of a ruthless fiend
   That trusting sister fell.
"She loved not wisely, but too well;"
   And was her fault forgiven?
Had she a friend to counsel *her?*
   Not one, except in Heaven.

The very brother that her voice
   Had pleaded most to save,
Heap'd curses on her hapless head
   And wish'd her in the grave.
The father who had seen her grow
   In beauty 'neath his eye,
Address'd her as a loathsome wretch,
   And cast her forth to die.

Bleak was the night, and as she walk'd
   Along the frozen street,
The outcast trembled as she felt
   The icy, chilling sleet.
She reach'd a lofty edifice,
   Made the hard porch her bed—

And as she sought the sleep of death,
"Forgive him, God," she said.

Next morning when the daylight broke,
Her stiffen'd corpse was found,
And hurriedly 'twas taken up
And put beneath the ground.
No prayer was said, no tear was shed
When she was laid in earth,
And he who wrought her fall is thought
A gentleman of worth.

Now, why is this? Should not the wretch
Who tramples in the dust
A young heart's purest offering,
Forever be accursed?
Should he not be compell'd to feel
The world's severest ban,
And meet the undisguised contempt
Of every honest man.

The wretched one who fell from grace
In Galilee of yore,
Was told by Him who died for us
To go and sin no more.
But now, if woman steps aside,
Society will cry,
"Sin on—there is no hope for thee!
Sin ever till you die!"

J

THE DRUNKARD'S DREAM.

THE drunkard lay on his bed of straw
In a poverty-stricken room—
And near him his wife and children three
Sat shivering in their misery
And weeping amid the gloom.

And as he slept, the drunkard dream'd
Of happy days gone by,
When he wooed and won a maiden fair
With rosy cheeks and golden hair,
And heavenly, soft-blue eye.

Again he wander'd near the spot
Where Mary used to dwell,
And heard the warbling of the birds
His darling loved so well,
And caught the fragrance of the flowers
That blossom'd in the dell.

Again he at the altar stood
And kiss'd his blushing bride,
And gazing on her beauty, felt
His bosom swell with pride,
And thought no prince could rival him,
With Mary at his side.

The drunkard's wife is brooding o'er
   The happy long ago—
In mute despair she sighs and rocks
   Her body to and fro.
He *dreams*—she *thinks*—yet both their thoughts
   In the same channel flow.

But now upon the drunkard's brow
   A look of horror dwells,
And of his fearful agony
   Each feature plainly tells—
Some hideous scene which wakes despair,
   His dream of bliss dispels.

Upon him glares a monster now
   With visage full of ire,
And yelling fiends with ribald songs
   Replace the feather'd choir,
And the pure water of the spring
   Is turn'd to liquid fire.

And as the red flames leap and roar
   Around the brooklet's brink,
The fiends a flaming goblet raise
   And urge the wretch to drink,
While overhead the stars fade out
   And all is black as ink.

"Drink, comrade, drink!" the demons cry.
   "Come to our banquet—come!
This is the fitting draught for those
   Who sell their souls for rum!"
No word the drunkard speaks, but stares
   As he were stricken dumb.

And now they point him to the brook,
And cry, "See, drunkard! see!
Amid yon flames are struggling
Your wife and children three,
And in their terror and despair,
They call for help on thee!"

He rush'd to aid them, but at once
The demons block'd his way,
And then he sank upon his knees
In agony, to pray;
But palsied was his tongue, and he
Could no petition say.

The drunkard writhed and from his brow
Cold perspiration broke,
As round the forms of those he loved
Curl'd up the flame and smoke,
And, shrieking in his agony,
The wretched man awoke.

He glared around with frenzied eyes—
His wife and children three
Sat shivering in their tatter'd rags
In abject misery,
And wept outright to look upon
His waking agony.

A pause—a sigh—and reason's light
Again did on him beam,
And springing to his feet, he cried,
"Thank God, 'twas but a dream,
And I, perhaps, may yet regain
My fellow-man's esteem!"

Then reaching forth his trembling hand,
He from the table took
A mother's gift when he was wed—
The good God's Holy Book;
And while his loved ones knelt around,
A solemn vow he took.

"So help me God, I ne'er again
Will touch the poison'd bowl
Which ruins health and character,
And steeps in guilt the soul,
And swells the fearful list of names
Affix'd to Satan's scroll!

"Help me, O Lord! to keep this oath—
To shun each vicious den
Wherein I'd feel the tempter's power
To make me sin again!"
And from his sobbing wife's white lips
Arose a loud "Amen!"

And then on her wan visage beam'd
A smile of joy once more,
And, clinging to her husband's neck,
She kiss'd him o'er and o'er,
And wept such happy tears as she
Had never wept before.

* * * * * *

He kept his oath, and from that time
Their home did Heaven seem;
No discord now—sweet peace was theirs,
And love their only theme.
And daily both gave thanks to God
Who sent the Drunkard's Dream.

THE BEGGAR-GIRL'S COMPLAINT.

"OLD Santa Claus has come again!"
The rich man's children cry,
And health glows in their ruddy cheeks
As they run shouting by.
I do not envy them their toys,
Nor would I check their glee;
But oh! I wish that Santa Claus
Would visit Sue and me!

They say he's merry, kind, and free;
But I am very sure,
Though this may be his character,
He does not like the poor.
For if he did, he'd call on them,
And give them of his store,
Instead of striding coldly on
Past every poor man's door.

I do not want his pretty toys,
His candies or his fruits;
I'd rather have, by far, a frock
Or pair of winter boots,
Or a nice warm stove to sit by,
Or a bonnet for the street,
Or a pair of woollen stockings,
Or a loaf of bread to eat.

Oh! if *I* were old Santa Claus,
I know what I would do;
I'd visit rich men's houses,
But I'd visit poor homes too.
And if I bless'd the rich man's child
With toys and dainties sweet,
I'd give the poor warm clothes to wear,
And food enough to eat.

I'd go to every lonely hut.
And every palace grand,
And scatter presents everywhere
With an unsparing hand.
And Christmas morning, when the bells
Gave out a joyful sound,
Not one sad face or bleeding heart
Should in the world be found.

Oh! if I were old Santa Claus,
I'd make all sad homes bright;
Boys should not swear, and lie, and steal;
Nor parents drink and fight;
Nor should poor homeless wanderers
Be treated cruelly,
While plodding through the bleak, dark streets,
Like little Sue and me.

But I am not old Santa Claus;
I'm but a beggar-girl,
Who's buffeted and kick'd about,
In the great city's whirl.

Not one kind voice addresses me,
None heed the pangs I feel,
And so to keep myself alive
I have to beg and steal.

O men! who b'lieve that Christ the Lord
Was poor while on the earth,
Steel not your hearts against us
On the morning of His birth;
But as your well-clad little ones
Throng round you in their glee,
Give one kind thought to such poor waifs
As little Sue and me.

"SEEKING WARMTH, AND FINDING DEATH."

A TRUE INCIDENT.

'TWAS a fearful night in winter—
A night of snow and sleet—
When a beggar, worn and weary
Crept through the lonely street.
To better his condition
He had left fair Italy,
And thought to find a Heaven in
This land of liberty.

He was sick, and sore, and ragged,
  And penniless, and old,
And shiver'd like an aspen
  In the bitter, biting cold;
And he wonder'd why he hunger'd
  And went without a bed,
For he had heard that strangers here
  Could always earn their bread.

While passing by a lime-kiln,
  He felt the genial glow
Of heat upon the surface
  From the burning mass below;
And he look'd up into Heaven,
  Where the blessed Saviour dwells,
And, muttering a prayer, he sought
  A bed upon the shells.

And, as sleep stole upon him,
  He saw a vision bright—
A grand, majestic figure,
  Array'd in purest white;
His eyes were full of pity,
  And his face was free from guile,
And on his countenance there play'd
  A beatific smile.

"Poor wanderer!" the stranger said;
  "Neglected, sick, and lone!
My heart goes out to thee, for I
  Have want and sorrow known;
I, too, have felt, in all its force,
  Man's inhumanity;

I, too, have been a man of grief—
A wanderer like thee.

"But I will gently nurse thee,
And lull thy cares to rest;
I'll snatch thee from thy misery,
And warm thee in my breast;
I'll take thee to my Father's house,
And thou shalt happy be,
Nor shalt thou know another pang—
Say, wilt thou go with me?"

Those dulcet tones fell sweetly
Upon the beggar's ear;
He realized, with joy, that he
Beheld the Saviour dear;
And ere the glorious sunshine
Proclaim'd another day,
The beggar's soul had plumed its wings,
And sped with Christ away.

Next morning, on the lime-kiln
The blacken'd corpse was found;
And as, with ghastly faces,
The workmen gather'd round,
They said to one another,
As they gazed, with bated breath:
"He came in here to look for warmth,
And in its stead found death!"

THE FELON'S LAST NIGHT.

THE felon lay in his gloomy cell,
His keeper sat close by;
The doom'd wretch knew, alas! too well,
That he must surely die
Before another sun should set;
And yet how strange that he
Should all his dread of death forget,
And slumber tranquilly!

He dream'd of childhood's happy hours
He heard the robin sing,
And cull'd again the sweet wild flowers
That blossom'd near the spring;
He saw his mother's look of pride,
And felt the same sweet joy
As when he frolick'd by her side,
A sinless, happy boy.

Again he linger'd on the green,
And cast his eyes about
In search of little Eveleen,
When irksome school was out;
Again he saw her sunny smile,
Her artless, bashful look,
And kiss'd her rosy cheek the while
They wander'd by the brook.

The sleeper's heart was all aglow
With innocent delight,
Nor dream'd he that a shade of woe
Could mar his vision bright;
A sweet smile wreath'd his haggard brow;
A prayer his thin lips moved,
"O Father! Thou hast bless'd me now—
I love, and I am loved!"

Ha! what a sound breaks on his ear!
The solemn prison bell
Rings out the summons loud and clear—
The prisoner's death-knell!
He springs erect! The look of joy
Has vanish'd from his brow!
His dream is o'er; the sinless boy
Is a doom'd felon now!

"Back! back!" he cried, with eyes agleam;
"Too soon the bell they toll!
I cannot die with that sweet dream
Yet ling'ring in my soul!
Back! back! Ere ye take me away
Through yonder prison door,
For Christ's sake grant me leave to stay
On earth one hour more!"

In vain the felon shrieks aloud,
And struggles to get free;
They drag him forth before the crowd
Around the gallows-tree.

The fatal noose is round his neck:
　A priest is standing near,
Beseeching him the cross to take,
　And banish every fear.

A moment's pause. The felon stands
　Like one in dreadful doubt;
Then clenching fast his bony hands,
　Defiantly shrieks out:
"Begone, vile priest! I spit at thee!
　I will not kiss the rod!
I b'lieve not in thy mummery!
　Away! there is no God!

"You say I'm doom'd! Ha! ha! 'tis well!
　No other world I fear—
I cannot meet a fiercer hell
　Than I have suffer'd here!"
The cap was drawn, the trap was sprung,
　And on the gallows-tree
The felon's lifeless body swung;
　His soul from earth was free,

NEW-YEAR'S EVE.

AT the close of a bitter cold day,
　When the snow on the frozen ground lay
A poor woman's child,
With a face wan and mild,

In a garret was passing away.
Gaunt hunger,
Dread hunger,
Had stolen the bloom from his cheek,
And his mother sat there,
With a look of despair,
To catch what her darling might speak.

"Come closer, dear mother," he said,
"And lay your soft hand on my head,
And tell me once more
Of that other bright shore
Where we never shall hunger for bread."
"Hush, darling!
Peace, darling!"
She raised him to lull him to rest,
And she brush'd the soft hair
From his forehead so fair,
But he died as he lay on her breast.

The morning broke joyous and clear,
'Twas the first of the opening year;
But the shouts of gay boys,
And the cannon's rude noise,
Fell unheard on that poor mother's ear.
Oh! hear it!
Oh! heed it!
Ye wealthy, well clothed, and well fed,
In that season of joy
A mother and her boy
Had perish'd for the want of bread.

POEMS OF COMEDY.

THE SURPRISE PARTY.

JOHN PINCHBECK lived on Murray Hill,
The upper-crust among,
He had a healthy bank account,
His wife was fair and young—
He'd earn'd a handsome competence
By selling hides and leather—
His head was level and his heart
As light as any feather.

But John's wife, pretty though she was,
And sociable and free,
Was fond of taking on French airs
When in society.
To see the lady in her silks
And diamonds array'd
'Twas hard to b'lieve she once had been
A simple dairy maid.

But so it was—and one fine day
A couple stout and jolly—
Zeke Soper and his wife—came down
To see their darling Polly.
For Polly was the lady's name
When at her spinning-wheel,
But now she'd changed it to Pauline,
As being more genteel.

"Oh, lawful sakes!" Zeke's wife cried out,
When she the mansion stood in,
"I hope I never more may see
A bowl of hasty puddin'
If this ain't scrumpshious! Only see
The picters on the ceilin'!
As nat'ral as life! Why, Zeke,
I'm on the p'int o' squealin'!

"It's fresco, is it? Well, I vow
I'm drefful glad you told me!
And see the carpets and the cheers,
And sofys! Zekel, hold me!
I'm nigh a bustin' with amaze!
I really am! Why, Polly,
With all these fixins 'round you, gal,
You must be awful jolly!

"It's mighty fine! But, goodness me!
Zeke, see them naked figgers
A standin' on the mantel-piece!
They make me blush, by jiggers!
You say they're noble works of art,
And great folks come to view 'em?
Well, Polly, dear, if I was you
I'd put some clothes onto 'em!

"What's that you say? Pauline's your name?
Good gracious me, what folly!
Why, wern't I by, you silly thing,
When you was christen'd Polly?

And if the name was good enough
  For your dear, blessed mother,
It's good enough for you, and I
  Sha'n't call you any other!

"But speakin' of your christenin', Poll,
  To me it is bewilderin'
That you've been married seven years
  And ain't had any children.
Your ma had twelve and I've had eight—
  Now, Polly, dear, confess it,
A house, though grand, ain't worth a snap
  Without a babe to bless it.

"What's that you say? You wish I'd try
  To speak with more propriety—
That havin' babes is frown'd upon
  By folks in good society?
Jerusalem! But that beats all!
  It's contrary to natur'!
Society is dead agin
  The law of the Creator!

"I've got a kind of idea, Poll,
  That you the Lord are grievin'—
Depend upon it, you can't take
  Your fashions up to Heaven.
You've kept from havin' babies,
  But the Lord you cannot cozen,
And at the awful judgment day
  You'll wish you'd had a dozen.

"But, deary me I'm tired out!
  My bones are ackin' cruel—
Come, Polly, show us to our room—
  I'd like a bowl of gruel.
And can't you get some bone-set tea
  And mustard for a body.
And a warm hand-iron for my feet?
  And Zeke would like some toddy!"

* * * * * *

Next evening Mrs. Pinchbeck thus
  Address'd her lord and master:
"Oh, husband, how can we survive
  This terrible disaster?
I'll die—I know I shall—if aunt
  And uncle with us tarry
Till they are seen by proud Miss Sharp
  And jealous Mrs. Barry.

"Such a disgrace! Just think of it!
  This morning at the table
The servants, though afraid to laugh
  Aloud, were scarcely able
To hide their mirth, when Uncle Zeke,
  By Aunt Jerusha follow'd,
Pick'd up the half-fill'd finger bowl
  And all the water swallow'd!"

Just then the hall-bell rang aloud,
  And soon a summons hearty
Smote on the lady's startled ear,
  "Ha, Pinchbeck! Here's a party!

We've come to give you a surprise—
 We know you'll be delighted
And welcome us right cordially,
 Though we were not invited!"

Poor Mrs. Pinchbeck! How was she
 The dreadful blow to parry?
She heard the voices of her friends,
 Miss Sharp and Mrs. Barry.
And many others whom she knew
 Delighted to perplex her,
And who would rummage high and low
 To scandalize and vex her.

"Friends!" cried the lady, "welcome all—
 I'm glad to see you, really!
Just pass down to the dining-room
 And use the closets freely
But please don't come up stairs, for we
 Two friends are entertaining—
Distinguish'd persons from abroad—
 Both nervous and complaining!"

Oh, horror! Even as she spoke,
 A voice that made her shiver
Came from above, "Oh, Zeke!" it cried,
 "That sirup for my liver!
I've left it in the room below—
 I cannot do without it—
Besides, there's company down stairs—
 Let's go and ask about it!"

Ere Mrs. Pinchbeck could prevent
  The act that her degraded,
The agèd couple merrily
  The dining-room invaded.
To make the matter worse, old Zeke
  Had taken too much toddy.
And felt that he was just as rich
  And grand as anybody.

"Why, how d' deu, good folks!" he cried,
  And then at Mrs. Barry
He wink'd and said, facetiously,
  "Lord, what a spread you carry!
Well, make yourselves to hum at once!
  Away with melancholy!
Hurrah! Let's have a straight-four dance!
  Jerushy, where is Polly?

"She needn't keep herself so shy
  Because she's got a fortin',
She was as poor as anyone
  'Fore Pinchbeck did his courtin'—
But this I'll always say for Poll—
  No other gal, I reckon,
Could ekal her at dairy work,
  At washin' or at bakin'.

"Ah, here she is! and Pinchbeck, too!
  Come, folks, bring on your fiddle,
And let us have an old time dance
  Up sides and down the middle!

Come, Polly, put your best licks in,
  Just as you used to do it
At all our frolics down to hum—
  Go on! I'll see yeou through it!"

Thus Uncle Zekel rattled on,
  And when his tongue had tired,
Old Aunt Jerush took up the theme
  With emulation fired.
She told her niece's history
  From childhood till she married,
While Mrs. Pinchbeck helpless stood
  And not a thrust was parried.

* * * * * *

Let's close the scene—a week pass'd by—
  The Pinchbecks, half demented,
Were writhing still when they received
  A note with perfume scented,
From Mrs. Barry. Thus it read:
  "To Mrs. Pinchbeck greeting:
Dear friend—the ladies of our set
  Are soon to have a meeting.

"Our object is to call upon
  And speak with Madame Herman
About the getting up in style
  Of our forthcoming German.
And if you'll send us the address
  Of your high-bred relations,
I'll see that they, as well as you,
  Are granted invitations!"

The moral of my story is
   That pride must have a tumble—
That those who in their wealth forget
   They once were poor and humble—
Who think they wear so close a mask
   That no one can detect it,
May come to grief with all their airs,
   E'en when they least expect it.

PERHAPS SO, BUT I DOUBT IT.

OLD Money Grub has piles of wealth,
   Yet toils like any digger;
Greed steels his heart and saps his health,
   But larger grows the figure.
He says religion is a lie,
   And men can do without it;
Will this pay when he comes to die?
   Perhaps so, but I doubt it.

And while old Grub hoards up his gold,
   Young Grub makes fast to spend it,
Resolved to sin till he is old—
   Then change his life and mend it.
But when age bids him right the wrong,
   Do you think he'll set about it?
Will long indulgence make him strong?
   Perhaps so, but I doubt it.

And Mrs. Grub, the miser's wife,
  Who prates of Mrs. Grundy,
And leads a very worldly life
  On every day but Sunday;
Will riches her the power give
  To conquer death or flout it?
Can she, by wishing, longer live?
  Perhaps so, but I doubt it.

And young Miss Grub, so full of airs,
  And devoid of candor,
So fond of shirking household cares,
  So very proud to slander;
Will Heaven her petition hear,
  However loud she shout it?
Will she rejoice when death draws near?
  Perhaps so, but I doubt it.

Will strife and anger lead to peace?
  Will riches bring contentment?
Will vice, by free indulgence, cease?
  Will hard words cure resentment?
When Heaven wills that we should bear
  Misfortune, can we rout it!
And is it wisdom to despair?
  Perhaps so, but I doubt it.

THE ROOT OF THE EVIL.

OLD Mr. Grump, the millionaire
Sat propp'd up in his easy chair,
Pretentious, pompous, stern and stout,
A martyr to *ennui* and gout.

A table near the old man stood,
On which were bits of dainty food;
Nor did the tempting spread-out lack
A bottle of old Cogniac.

While nibbling some delicious game,
The doctor he had summon'd came—
And laying back his frame to rest,
Grump thus the man of pills address'd:

"Now listen to me, Dr. Squill,
I wish you'd either cure or kill—
If you would have me use you civil,
Strike at the real root of my evil."

The doctor paused and thought awhile,
Then, with a very pleasant smile,
He raised his cane, and with one stroke
The well-fill'd brandy bottle broke.

OURS.

JOHN HAWTHORNE was a worthy man—
A farmer blythe and free;
He own'd two hundred acres,
And a widower was he.
His hands were hard with honest toil,
His intellect was sound;
And he possess'd the finest stock
In all the country 'round.

But John was discontented,
In spite of all his wealth—
His fruitful soil, his stock so rare,
His never-failing health—
The blooming, buxom Widow Green
Had set at him her cap,
And for his vast possessions now
He didn't care a rap.

And so it one day happen'd
That in his best array'd,
He sought the charming widow's cot,
And there before her laid
His heart, and hand, and fortune—
And is it strange to say
That she, the fair, bewitching dame,
Accepted them straightway?

The knot once tied so firmly
  That there could be no slip,
The happy couple started off
  Upon their bridal trip.
They visited Niagara,
  And Saratoga, too;
And o'er them, like a happy dream,
  The golden hours flew.

Alas, for human pleasure!
  The sunshine and the cloud
Will throw their light and shade alike
  On humble and on proud,
And even at the moment
  When love their bosoms stirr'd,
Their happiness was shatter'd
  By a simple little word.

"My love," said John, one morning,
  "Thou sharer of my bliss!"
(And here he gave his partner
  A sweet, ecstatic kiss)
"Now that I'm fairly settled
  With my darling little wife,
I think I'll sell my farm at once,
  And lead an easy life."

"Say *our* farm, my darling!"
  John's loving spouse replied.
John slightly frowned an instant
  Upon his charming bride.

"*My* farm, love," he repeated—
"I will not call it thine;
I grant you we are wedded,
But still the farm is *mine!*"

"*Our* farm!" "*My* farm!" "*Our* farm!"
"*My* farm!"
And thus the fight went on,
Till Mrs. Hawthorne No. 2
Attacked the luckless John
With teeth and nails together,
Till he was forced to yield—
He said, "*Our* farm!" and his fair bride
Was mistress of the field.

Now when this tired couple
To their rustic home return'd,
Was John Hawthorne unmindful
Of the lesson he had learn'd?
Was he resolved henceforward
The lady's boss to be?
Well, be not too impatient—
Wait awhile and we shall see.

"My dear, what are you looking for?"
Asked Mrs. H. one day.
"I'm looking for *our* razor, love!"
Her humble spouse did say.
"We have mislaid it somehow,
And our beard is getting long;
I daresay we shall find it
Our travelling traps among.

"Another thing, my darling—
  I'd really like to know
Where our slippers vanish'd to—
  Our bunions hurt us so!
And won't you, please, my own love,
  Insert a few strong stitches
In this bad rent a nail made
  In our best working breeches?"

And thus the lady's *dictum*
  Is heeded day by day,
And timid Mr. Hawthorne
  Has not a word to say;
Her firm determination
  His weak will overpowers—
She orders all to suit herself
  And everything is "*ours*."

The moral of my story
  All men can understand:
If a widower is anxious
  To secure a widow's hand,
It should be fairly understood,
  Before the knot is tied,
To whom the property belongs—
  To him or to his bride.

BE CAREFUL WHAT YOU WRITE.

OH, wealthy, toil-worn merchant,
With ever busy brain,
While poring o'er thy ledger
And counting loss and gain,
When tradesmen are complaining,
And money's very "tight,"
If ask'd for your endorsement,
Be careful what you write.

And you, excited lover,
Whose heart wells o'er with sighs,
Whose brain is dazed while gazing
In a pair of roguish eyes—
If you're impell'd by Cupid
A missive to indite,
When you sit down to pen your thoughts
Be careful what you write.

And thou, oh, wealthy graybeard—
A widower, mayhap—
Entranced by some gay widow
Who sets at you her cap—
Should she send you a letter
Which fills you with delight,
When you essay an answer,
Be careful what you write.

And let me caution thee, too,
  Thou man of passions strong,
When you are writhing under
  Some real or fancied wrong,
And longing to demolish
  Your adversary quite,
By sending him a letter,
  Be careful what you write.

And thou, oh, busybody,
  Whose never weary eye
Gleams greedily whenever
  A neighbor's fault you spy,
Your specious inuendoes
  May safely speak your spite;
But if you'd 'scape a lawsuit,
  Be careful what you write.

And thou, oh, gifted author,
  Whose ready, facile pen
Developes scenes and incidents
  Which thrill thy fellow men—
Let reason and morality
  Control thy fancy's flight—
Say nothing which may foster sin—
  Be careful what you write.

The memory of idle words
  Perhaps may pass away—
The evil they engender
  Be forgotten in a day;

But once in print, they may appear,
  Some guileless soul to blight,
When you have molder'd into dust—
  Be careful what you write.

Oh, ye who wield the mighty pen!
  Thrice happy is his lot
Who, "living, never wrote a line
  That, dying, he would blot."
No terrors of the dread beyond
  Can such a soul affright—
Then ye who furnish mental food,
  Be careful what you write.

THE LAW STUDENT.

A FORWARD youth just home from college,
  Where he was seeking legal knowledge,
Anxious his wisdom to display
His father thus address'd one day:
"Now, father, here's an apple—see—
Which I design to give to thee—
But so that none thy claim dispute,
And to despoil thee bring a suit,
I'll give it thee in legal way,
As thus—to wit—that is to say:

"I give you all and singular,
Without encumbrance, let, or bar,
My interest, title and estate—
Whether the same be small or great—
My present right and claim, and all
Advantage, whatsoe'er befall,
That apple in, for your own use,
With all its seed, skin, pulp and juice—
With all advantage and all right,
With power to sell, roast, cut or bite—
With power to eat or give away
At any hour, night or day,
In mouthfuls or in single gulp,
With all its seed, skin, juice and pulp.
Anything publish'd heretofore
Or hereinafter, less or more,
Or any instrument, deeds or deed
Made in the past or to succeed
Of what kind or nature countermanding
To the contrary, notwithstanding.
No man to cancel this need try—
Now, father, how is that for high?"

The puzzled sire scratch'd his head,
Then, with a sigh, he slowly said:
"I think, my bright son, that the law
Is like a pickerel's head, all jaw.
Now you may to the cellar go
And split wood—how is that for low?

THE JOLLY HERMIT.

LATE, while wand'ring through a forest,
Sad and grave,
Suddenly I saw before me
A hermit's cave.
Wearied out and faint with walking,
Full of care,
Sick at heart, and needing solace,
I enter'd there.

On a rude bench, fondly patting
A purring cat,
All his features beaming welcome,
The hermit sat.
Very old he was, and hoary,
But merrily
He laugh'd aloud, and kindly bade me
Seated be.

"Tell me," I said, "thou hoary hermit,
So old and poor,
What dost thou find on earth that worketh
Affliction's cure?
There's naught around thy hut but telleth
Of misery,
And yet thy piping voice is cheery
And full of glee."

"I'll tell thee, boy," he said, and gayly
His beard he twirl'd.
"The thing's explain'd in one brief sentence:
I've left the world!
When I was in it I had trouble,
And felt, I trow,
As badly, oft, and as dejected
As you do now.

"You will not yet essay the cure, boy,
Too young are you,
And heart-sorrows are but transient
When life is new;
But if you'd 'scape the many trials
Which me befell,
Take from me these brief precepts,
And heed them well.

"Make love the basis of your actions
Invariably;
But let it be *self-love*—no other
Can wholesome be.
Trust thou no man, and love no woman—
Hard task indeed!—
But, sooth, if you neglect this warning
Your heart *must* bleed.

"Look to it that you favor no one—
Be this your boast;
For those who are your greatest debtors
Will hate you most.

Live for yourself; be shrewd and wary;
Shut up you heart
And close your eyes to all that suffer
Affliction's smart.

"For forty years I loved to practice
Sweet charity,
But found in every one I aided
An enemy;
Now I am old, and wise, and happy,
And free from strife—
And thus, boy, you may conquer
The ills of life."

"Avaunt!" I cried, "thou hoary hermit!
Thy words appall!
Thou'dst turn the milk of human kindness
To bitter gall!
The sweetest jets that issue from life's fountain
Are faith and love—
In deeds of Heav'nly charity we foretaste
The bliss above."

"Ha! ha!" then gayly laugh'd the hermit:
"*My plan is true!*
I've proved it to my satisfaction,
And so will you;
And all the diff'rence between us
Under the sun
Is this, *that I am over eighty—*
You're twenty-one."

THE TINKER'S MISTAKE.

ATTENTION, friends, and I will tell
What once a luckless wight befell—
A travelling tinker, named John Drew,
Who daily tramp'd the country through.

A shiftless vagabond was John,
Who little reck'd how he got on;
Enough to eat, a bed when tired,
Was all the wealth which he desired.

And, then, to give the man his due,
He was to friendship firm and true;
His motto was, "Man is my brother,
And one good turn deserves another."

Alert he was, and wide awake;
But once he made a sad mistake,
Which bow'd him down with shame and grief,
From which he vainly sought relief.

Thus runs the story: John, one day,
Had tramp'd a long and weary way,
When a neat road-side inn he saw,
And panting halted at the door.

"Landlord," John cried, "my worthy friend,
Any old pots or pans to mend?"
"Yes," said the host with clouded brow,
"But money's rather scarce just now."

"I want no cash," the tinker said;
"For supper, breakfast, and a bed,
I'll do the work, and think it fun."
"Done!" cried the landlord, "double done!"

The tinker labor'd with a will,
And back'd by honesty and skill,
Ere scarce one toilsome hour had sped,
He'd finish'd, supp'd, and gone to bed.

John Drew enjoy'd his night's repose,
And in the morning he arose,
And having breakfasted, he sped
Unto the worthy host, and said,

"Landlord, my warmest thanks are due
For the great kindness shown by you;
You certainly can keep an inn
As well as I can patch up tin.

"But still it does not seem to pay,
And you should find some other way
To help increase your slender store,
And keep the gaunt wolf from your door."

"The inn pays not," the landlord said,
"But then I have another trade.
I am the village glazier here,
And all *that* brings is profit clear."

"Well, good luck to you!" utter'd John,
As with his budget he trudged on;
"I sha'n't forget, my generous brother,
That one good turn deserves another!"

Deep gratitude felt stout John Drew,
The feeling thrill'd him through and through,
And as the village church he pass'd
A brilliant idea held him fast.

He paused awhile in thought profound,
Then cast a cautious glance around;
Then mutter'd firmly, "I will do it,
E'en though I'm caught and made to rue it!"

Then picking up a stone, John Drew
A window sent it crashing through;
And then stone after stone deliver'd
Till every pane of glass was shiver'd.

Back to the inn went John once more,
And soon the landlord stood before,
And striving hard his mirth to smother,
Cried, "One good turn deserves another!

"You gave me work my bread to earn,
And I the favor now return;
O generous host! upon my soul
No window in the church is whole.

"I've smash'd each one, kind friend, and you,
Will soon have work enough to do.
For you're a glazier, and you know
The work won't from the village go!

The landlord glared at John amazed:
Then like one by misfortune crazed,
He caught him by the throat and swore
Such oaths as ne'er were heard before.

"Wretch!" he exclaim'd, "why did you so?
Your *kindness* works my overthrow!
I am the only glazier here,
But keep the church whole by the year!"

MORAL.

My moral plainly has this end:
Take no wrong means to help a friend.
For if from right's clear path you swerve,
You'll hurt the cause you fain would serve.

MAN AND THE LOWER ANIMALS.

ONE day when business was dull,
And I had time to spare,
In philosophic mood I sought
A crowded thoroughfare.
And there I idly took my stand
And close attention gave
To studying the heads of those
Who pass'd me on the pave.

"Now, there," I whisper'd to myself,
"A bull-dog nature goes—
His head is small, his neck is thick,
His eye with anger glows.
His chest is broad, his limbs are strong,
His look is full of spite,
'Tis very evident that he,
In fighting takes delight."

And now one who reminds me
Of a mastiff, passes by,
With deep bass voice, square-hanging jaw,
And watchful, eager eye.
He may be a detective
Of energy and skill,
Who has the bull-dog's strength and pluck
Without his wish to kill.

Here comes a human greyhound—
A fellow lithe and lank,
Lean-ribb'd and sharp of voice—
He is a runner for a bank.
He keeps the chase up constantly,
With never weary feet,
Nor does he stop to bother with
The "lame ducks" on the street.

And now a small man passes by—
A nervous little chap—
Restless, alert, bold, confident,
And sharp as a steel trap.
I fancy he's a man of law,
Presumptuous and defiant,
He's like a terrier who has
A fat rat for a client.

Here comes a man with large mild eyes,
And glossy, curly hair—
A figure most symmetrical—
A brave and honest air.

He's like the noble Newfoundland—
  The favorite of all—
Willing to peril life itself
  When roused by duty's call.

Then comes a man who carries
  The visage of an owl,
And an oily, pig-faced man who walks
  With under-hanging jowl.
A timid, sheep-faced man, who seems
  Of everything in awe;
An hirsute man, with lion mane,
  And fierce, terrific roar:

A stubborn, dull, bull-headed man—
  A man of serpent head—
A man who has the tiger's look,
  With eye-balls fierce and red.
In short the lower animals
  Are met with everywhere,
In those we choose to study
  On a crowded thoroughfare.

THE IRISH FRENCHMAN.*

AN English ship, by some mischance,
Once founder'd on the coast of France;
But all her crew—at least a score
Of stalwart sailors—reach'd the shore.

At first, of course, they could but fret;
But sailors are a jolly set,
And seldom long will entertain
A grief on either land or main.

So, when they'd mourn'd an hour or two,
With one consent the hapless crew
Ceased murm'ring and began to think
About securing food and drink.

Ere long they plenty had to eat—
A good supply of fish and meat—
But how to cook it knew they not,
Since they had neither pan nor pot.

Soon spoke the captain, with a cheer,
"See yonder smoke! A cot is near
Where we could borrow what we seek,
If we'd a man who French could speak."

* It is only proper to state that this Poem was suggested by a story entitled "The Gridiron," which may be found in Samuel Lover's "Irish Stories and Legends." It may not be as well told, perhaps, as in the original prose, but the reader may take it for what it is worth.

"Spake Frinch!" a sailor quick replied—
An Irishman named Pat McBride—
"I learn'd the language years ago,
While I was shtopping at Bordeaux!"

"Have patience, byes dear, ivery one,
While I to yonder cabin run,
And in a jiffy yez'll see,
I'll bring a griddle back wid me!"

Away he bounded, like a deer,
And when he drew the cottage near,
A grey-hair'd Frenchman he espied,
Who stood the cabin door beside.

"Och, polly voo Fransay, monseer!"
He said, with a complaisant leer.
"Oui, monsieur!" the man replied,
As he the sailor keenly eyed.

"Well, thin, a griddle I would borrow—
I'll let yez have it back to-morrow.
Perhaps I'll fetch it back before"—
The Gaul replied, "*Je n'entends pas!*" *

"It isn't yer long tongs I wish,"
Said Pat. "I want to cook some fish,
Me friends are yonder on the shore."
The Frenchman said, "*Je n'entends pas!*"

Pat stopp'd awhile and scratch'd his head,
And then again he loudly said,
"Och, polly voo Fransay—d'ye hear?"
The Gaul replied, "*Oui, monsieur!*"

---

* "I don't understand!" Pronounced "Zhar nontong par."

Poor Paddy now began to rant—
"Your griddle, not your tongs, I want!
So bring it out, and hould yer jaw!"
The Gaul replied, "*Je n'entends pas!*"

"D'ye mind!" said Pat, in accents gruff,
"I've borne your nonsense long enough—
And I'll not bear it any more!"
Still cried the Gaul, "*Je n'entends pas!*"

"Take that!" cried Paddy, with a frown,
As he the hapless Gaul knock'd down;
But still the astonished man did roar,
"*Je n'entends pas! Je n'entends pas!*"

Back to his comrades Paddy flew,
And soon around him flock'd the crew—
"What luck! What luck, Pat?" cried they all.
"Troth," answered Pat, "no luck at all!

"Byes, dear, d'ye see, we've fallen among
Frinchmen who can't shpake their own tongue;
Bedad, to me it seems a riddle,
They say 'long tongs' instead of griddle!"

MORAL.

My moral plainly all can see—
No one should a pretender be;
Fór mere pretense, when put to test,
Is worse than ignorance confess'd.

POEMS FOR MUSIC.

THERE'S GOOD IN THE WORLD.

THERE'S good in this beautiful world, I am thinking,
In spite of what splenetic cynics may say;
Its sweets we forget, while its bitter we're drinking—
In the gloom of its night we lose sight of its day.
When the storm breaks upon us awakening terror,
We utter our useless complainings aloud,
Forgetting the while, in our short-sighted error,
The sun that shines brightly behind every cloud.

There is good in the world—e'en adversity teaches
A lesson, if we will but read it aright—
It shows us our friends and exposes the leeches
Who only cling to us when all things are bright.
Oh, when the dark waves of misfortune o'erflow us,
How ready are some our mistakes to condemn—
'Tis only 'neath fortune's bright smile some friends know us,
And in our misfortune we learn to know them.

There is good in the world—ah, yes, never doubt it—
The unlucky stroke that awakens despair,
May come with a halo of friendship about it
To soften the blow and to lessen your care.
Oh, is it not sweet, when the world seems so weary,
And poverty stands like a wolf at your door,
To find a true man in the wilderness dreary,
Whose friendship you never had tested before!

And such men there are, making life's arid places
To bloom like a garden—to brighten and bless—
Their hearts overflowing with love for all races—
Their ears ever keen for the cry of distress.
Oh, temple of brotherhood! Blest is thy portal!
The ray from thy lamp to no spot is confined,
But shines through the world, giving each wretched mortal
More trust in his Maker, more faith in his kind.

STAND TO THE RIGHT.

STAND to the right, whate'er your condition,
Even though friends may to enemies turn—
Better have enemies in a just mission,
Than a dark record of infamy earn.
Friendship that's fickle is not worth preserving,
Wealth gain'd by fraud and deceit is a curse—
Stand by the right, then, undaunted, unswerving,
Poverty's bad, but dishonesty's worse.

Stand to the right—it were folly to barter
Self-independence for station or gain—
Better to virtue and truth fall a martyr
Than win a success mix'd with sorrow and pain.
An unsullied heart and a conscience approving
Are worth all the wealth that the world can bestow—
Stand by the right—be forgiving and loving,
Asking no favor and fearing no foe.

Stand to the right! 'Tis the best and the surest—
Wrong may appear for a while to succeed—
But he is most happy whose heart is the purest—
A self-condemn'd sinner is wretched indeed.
Hate and detraction in vain may assail thee
If thou art pure when their arrows they cast—
Honor and rectitude never will fail thee—
Stand to the right and you'll triumph at last.

WEAR NO ANGER ON THY BROW.

COME, and sit thee down beside me—
If I've pain'd thee tell me how—
Nay, my darling, do not chide me—
Wear no anger on thy brow.
Yours is not a face for ire—
Yours no tongue a war to wage—
Yours no eye to flash forth fire—
Yours no heart to cherish rage.
Come, then, sit thee down beside me—
If I've pained thee tell me how—
Nay, my darling, do not chide me—
Wear no anger on thy brow.

Once in honeyed words sincerest—
Words I never can forget—
You confess'd you loved me, dearest,
And I know you love me yet.

And the depth of my devotion
  I have spoken o'er and o'er,
And I'll feel the sweet emotion
  'Till my term of life is o'er.
    Come, then, sit thee down beside me—
      If I've pain'd thee, tell me how—
    Nay, my darling, do not chide me—
      Wear no anger on thy brow.

CREEP CLOSE TO MY HEART, O MY DARLING.

CREEP close to my heart, O my darling!
  And put up your lips for a kiss,
And tell me what joy in existence
  Can equal a moment like this?
I know that time flies while I clasp thee,
  But on let his chariot roll;
While near thee, he loses his power,
  Thou life-giving light of my soul!

Creep close to my heart, O my darling!
  I envy no king on his throne,
While thus in sweet rapture I hold thee,
  My dear one! my treasure! my own!
Oh! what would the world be without thee?
  Who else could my lone heart delight?
How 'twould darken my life should I lose thee,
  Thou day-star that rose on my night!

Creep close to my heart, O my darling!
And tell me thy hopes and thy fears;
And shouldst thou feel sorrow while talking,
I'll soon kiss away thy bright tears.
Come, tell me again that you love me,
That nothing shall tear us apart,
While I banish thy fears with my kisses—
Thou radiant queen of my heart!

BEAUTIFUL BESSIE.

BEAUTIFUL Bessie, young, joyous, and sweet
As the flowers that bloom in her sylvan retreat,
Is weaving a coronet, fragrant and gay,
For she has been chosen as Queen of the May.
Yet she heeds not the rosy-cheek'd youth who stands near
And timidly whispers his love in her ear;
A beau from the city has turn'd her weak head,
And she laughs at the rustic who asks her to wed.

Chorus—O wicked vanity!
Fatal insanity!
What will it cost?
Pride has o'erpower'd her!
Sin has devour'd her!
Bessie is lost!

Beautiful Bessie, once Queen of the May,
Has thrown her sweet wreath of fresh flowers away,

And changed her old home and her humble attire—
Denied her low birth and resolved to climb higher.
And now in a mansion of glitter and show
She drinks in the words of her grand city beau;
Gay is the laughter that breaks from her lips,
Bright are her eyes as the clear wine she sips.

Chorus—O wicked vanity!
Fatal insanity!
What will it cost?
Pride has o'erpower'd her!
Sin has devour'd her!
Bessie is lost!

Beautiful Bessie is out on the street;
Cold blows the night breeze, and sharp is the sleet;
But the rude tempest brings with it no smart,
'Tis not so keen as the storm in her heart.
Brief was her gay dream, and when she awoke,
Sad was her waking—her trusting heart broke.
And ere another day glides o'er her head,
Beautiful Bessie will sleep with the dead.

Chorus—O wicked vanity!
Fatal insanity!
What has it cost?
Pride has o'erpower'd her!
Sin has devour'd her!
Bessie is lost!

COME BACK TO ME.

TOO long have we been parted—
Come back to me!
I'm lonely, broken-hearted—
Come back to me!
I tread familiar bowers,
But scentless are the flowers,
And weary are the hours—
Come back to me!

Think of your promise broken—
Come back to me!
Your words of love once spoken—
Come back to me!
Hearts truly pledged forever
No thoughtless word should sever,
The past we'll think of never—
Come back to me!

I've loved since first I met thee—
Come back to me!
I never can forget thee—
Come back to me!
With looks of love I'll meet thee,
With words of love I'll greet thee;
Relent, then, I entreat thee—
Come back to me!

SHOULD FORTUNE FROWN.

SHOULD fortune frown,
Be not cast down;
The sailor on the ocean,
When skies grow dark,
Prepares his bark
To meet the storm's commotion.
And so should we,
On life's rude sea,
Be ever up and ready
To meet each storm
That comes along
With courage firm and steady.

Strive all you can,
Work like a man
To compass what you would do;
Then if you fail,
At fate don't rail,
You've done all that you could do;
Hope on, hope ever—
Dejection never
Yet won rank or station;
And toil, though vain,
At least will gain
Kind friendship's approbation.

After a shower,
The bright-hued flower
    Will only look the brighter;
So should the heart
By sorrow's smart
    Be render'd purer, lighter.
No man should fear
The ills met here,
    With providence above him;
A constant mind,
A soul resign'd,
    And one true heart to love him.

FRIENDLESS NELLY.

LITTLE Nelly, pale with hunger,
    Wanders through the street,
Heavy is her heart with sorrow,
    Weary are her feet.
Penniless she journeys homeward,
    Shivering with dread,
For her father is a drunkard,
    And her mother's dead.
What a sad, sad lot for Nelly,
    Nelly meek and mild!
Heavenly Father, oh! in pity
    Shield the drunkard's child.

Nelly's eyes are large and lustrous,
Golden is her hair,
And she has a sweet expression,
Nelly's very fair.
But the child's unearthly beauty,
That should be her crown,
All too soon may prove the burden
That will drag her down.
What a sad, sad lot for Nelly,
Nelly meek and mild!
Heavenly Father, oh! in pity
Shield the drunkard's child.

Nelly's character is spotless,
She is pure as snow;
Can she, in the wicked city,
Keep forever so?
Sin, and sorrow, and temptation,
Still her steps pursue;
Motherless, with no adviser,
What will Nelly do?
What a sad, sad lot for Nelly,
Nelly meek and mild!
Heavenly Father, oh! in pity
Shield the drunkard's child.

WOMAN.

A HEALTH to the lass with the laughing blue eye,
That seems to have borrow'd its hue from the sky—
Where young love is constantly feeding his flame,
And virtue sits blocking the entrance to shame.
Who weeps with the mourning and laughs with the gay,
Who can comfort old age or with infancy play,
Who quarrels with no one, but sticks to her creed—
Here's to her, for she is a woman indeed!

And here's to the girl with the lustrous black eye,
Who one moment may laugh and the next moment sigh;
Whose heart is a casket of joy and of grief,
And the first knows no limit, the last no relief.
Who deeply doth love, but as deeply can hate—
A Christian, and yet a believer in fate—
Who for pity will weep, or in anger will kill—
Here's her health—she is one of the softer sex still!

Here's to the coquette with the optic of gray,
Who will never say yes, but can hardly say nay;
Who falls dead in love with each gay beau she sees,
But can never find one for a long time to please.
Who is anxious to marry, and yet is afraid;
Who lives a young ninny, and dies an old maid;
Though blameful her follies it must be confess'd,
Yet her health—she's a woman as well as the rest.

In fine, here's to woman—the large and the small,
The lean and the fleshy, the short and the tall,
The dark eye, the blue eye, the hazel and gray,
The cheerful and sullen, the grave and the gay.
I care not how faulty their natures may be—
They are women—which fact is sufficient for me;
As mother, friend, sister, maid, widow, or wife,
They are God's best gift to man, the consolers of life.

THE OLD KNICKERBOCKER'S SONG.

GIVE me the good old days again,
When hearts were true and manners plain;
When boys were boys till fully grown,
And baby belles were never known;
When doctors' bills were light and few,
And lawyers had not much to do;
When honest toil was well repaid,
And theft had not become a trade.

Give me the good old days again,
When cider was not called champagne,
And round the fire in wintry weather,
Nuts and dry jokes were crack'd together;
When girls their lovers battled for
With seeds from juicy apple's core,
While mam and dad looked on with glee,
Well pleased their merriment to see.

Give me the good old days again,
When only healthy stock was slain;

When flour was pure, and milk was sweet,
And sausages were fit to eat;
When children early went to bed,
And ate no sugar on their bread;
When lard was not turned into butter,
And tradesmen only truth would utter.

Give me the good old days again,
When women were not proud and vain;
When fashion did not sense outrun,
And tailors had no need to dun;
When wealthy parents were not fools,
And common sense was taught in schools;
When hearts were warm and friends were true,
And Satan had not much to do.

Give me the good old days again,
Ere fraud and violence had reign;
When voters did not look for booty,
And judges dared to do their duty.
When patriots were not bought and sold,
But work'd for country—not for gold;
When every citizen could vote
Without a dagger at his throat.

Give me the good old days again,
When our exchequer felt no drain;
When men in place to "grind their axes,"
Swell'd not our public debts and taxes.
When alms-house keepers had some feeling,
And lived in clover without stealing.
Alas! alas! I sigh in vain
To see those good old days again.

YOU'LL WEEP WHEN I AM DEAD.

SMILE while thou canst, be gay and unheeding,
 Riches and splendor at last are thine own;
Strive to forget that a true heart is bleeding,
 Proud in its anguish, but wretched and lone.
And when the clouds of despair hover o'er thee,
 When the false friends of thy summer have fled,
Then will my sorrowing shade flit before thee;
 False to me living, you'll weep when I'm dead.

Blithesome and free in life's morning you found me,
 Sorrow had never o'ershadow'd my brow;
Bright fell the sunlight of sweet peace around me—
 Where, O thou fickle one! where is it now?
Gone! like the light on the verge of the ocean,
 Raised by false hands to allure the doom'd bark—
Suddenly quench'd 'mid the wild storm's commotion,
 Leaving the wreck'd ones to grope in the dark.

Gay is thy dream, but soon comes the dawning,
 When thou'lt awaken to sorrow and shame;
Wealth fleeth like the light mists of the morning,
 And there's no bubble more empty than fame.
Ah! then, when clouds of despair hover o'er thee,
 When the false friends of thy summer have fled,
My mournful shade will, I know, flit before thee—
 False to me living, you'll weep when I'm dead.

WHAT ARE THE SAD WAVES SAYING?

WHAT are the sad waves saying
Evermore,
As they in ceaseless playing
Kiss the shore?
They are saying,
In their swaying,
O'er and o'er:
"On the shore we're dying—
Time is onward flying—
And life's waves are rolling
Beyond man's controlling
Evermore!"

What are the sad waves saying
Evermore,
As they in ceaseless playing
Kiss the shore?
They are saying,
In their swaying,
O'er and o'er:
"Joy has no to-morrow,
Life is full of sorrow,
And the restless ocean
Types the soul's commotion
Evermore."

What are the sad waves saying
Evermore,
As they in ceaseless playing
Kiss the shore?
They are saying,
In their swaying,
O'er and o'er:
"O ye lovers walking,
Fondly, sweetly talking
On the strand,
Fervent vows, rose-tinted,
Are like lines imprinted
On the sand."

What are the sad waves saying
Evermore,
As they in ceaseless playing
Kiss the shore?
They are saying,
In their swaying,
O'er and o'er:
"Foolish boy or maiden,
Dreaming of sweet Aiden
On the shore,
Time will prove your treasures
And your keenest pleasures
Day-dreams—nothing more!"

WHY ART THOU COLD?

WHY art thou cold and careless while I'm near
thee?
Has thy vain heart proved recreant to me?
Dost thou seek other eyes and lips to cheer thee?
And art thou really anxious to be free?
With all my soul, then, let us kiss and sever,
I would not hold thee captive 'gainst thy will.
O thou once wildly loved! farewell forever,
Thy voice will ne'er again my pulses thrill.

Thou art false to me—another kneels before thee
To whisper love in thy too willing ear.
To swear that he forever will adore thee—
I hope for thy sake that he is sincere.
As for myself, I'm willing he should woo thee,
I'm willing thou shouldst call him all thine own,
I would not whisper one objection to thee;
I love thee not, my heart has callous grown.

'Tis vain to say that love, though scorn'd and slighted
Day after day, will suffer and live on;
By cold neglect the fondest love is blighted,
It lives not when its aliment is gone.
I loved thee once, and would have loved forever,
Hadst thou been true and loyal unto me;
The spell is broken—thou art free, and never
Shall my proud heart deplore the loss of thee.

CRAZY ESTELLE.

IN the great city she wanders alone;
None to befriend her—uncared for, unknown—
Muttering ever of joys that have fled,
Calling on some one who sleeps with the dead.
What her life's story is no one can tell—
She is known only as Crazy Estelle.
No one to pity her, none to caress—
God help the wanderer in her distress.

CHORUS.

No one to pity her, none to caress—
God help the wanderer in her distress!

Hopelessly lost in the city's vast throng,
Sadly she warbles a plaintive love-song;
Looking around her, but looking in vain,
For a loved face she will ne'er see again.
Wild is her dark eye and frenzied her air,
And her white brow is convulsed by despair;
But not a wicked thought enters her head,
She only seeks for a lover that's dead.

CHORUS.

No one to pity her, none to caress—
God help the wanderer in her distress!

What will become of her out in the street?
Heart-sick and foot-sore, no happy retreat;
Who will take care of her? Where can she go?
Wretched, forlorn, and o'erburden'd with woe.
No one on earth can the wanderer save,
And she will only find rest in the grave.
Guard her, bright angels, where'er she may tread,
Seeking in vain for her lover that's dead.

CHORUS.

No one to pity her, none to caress—
God help the wanderer in her distress!

THE LASS OF CLOVER LANE.

SWEET are the flowers which bloom around
The cot where I was born,
And sweet the melody of birds
That greet the early morn.
Sweet are the daisies and blue-bells
That gem the verdant plain,
But sweeter than all these to me,
My lass of Clover Lane.

There is no perfume like her breath,
Nor do the birds excel
The music of her merry laugh,
Clear as a silver bell,
Pure as a daisy wash'd with dew—
As modest, neat and plain—
The queen of love and beauty is
My lass of Clover Lane.

The city belle whose cheeks are red
   With artificial bloom,
And whose rich gems flash brilliantly
   In ball or concert-room,
May please the pamper'd man of wealth,
   Conceited, proud, and vain;
But I will pay my homage to
   The lass of Clover Lane.

My darling has no jewels rare,
   Nor can she boast of wealth;
But she is rich in innocence, sweet peace,
   And robust health.
She weeps with those oppress'd by woe,
   And at the couch of pain
She is an angel minister,
   My lass of Clover Lane.

So natural, so beautiful,
   So free from guile or art—
Oh! joy to press her to my breast,
   And wear her in my heart.
Should death my angel snatch from me,
   I'd never smile again;
My heart would wither should it lose
   The lass of Clover Lane.

MISCELLANEOUS POEMS.

A "CAPITAL" THEME.

THE burning rays of the midday sun
Pour down on the city's pave,
And 'neath its glare full many a one
Is hastening to the grave.
While Mammon sits in her cool retreat,
Far from the town's turmoil,
And cries with glee, "The dust and heat
Were made for the sons of toil!
Their muscle and bone
Are mine alone—
I use them at my will—
And what care I
How fast they die,
If they my coffers fill?"

A laborer from the giddy height
Of a ladder's topmost round,
Struck by the sun-ray's scorching blight,
Comes toppling to the ground.
And Capital takes of his wine a sup,
While looking on with a frown,
And says, "Our tenements must go up
If laborers do come down!"

Their muscle and bone
Are mine alone—

I use them at my will—
And what care I
How fa3t they die,
If they my coffers fill?"

A widow, wild with grief, bends o'er
The corpse of a stalwart man,
Who but a little while before
His earthly course had ran.
And Capital, viewing the woman's distress,
Cries out in a tone of ire,
"Canals and railroads must progress
If laborers do expire!"
Their muscle and bone
Are mine alone—
I use them at my will—
And what care I
How fast they die,
If they my coffers fill?"

Again, what dreadful sight has made
That mother's cheek to blench?
Her son has dug with pick and spade
A grave as well as a trench!
And Capital cries, with mirthful eyes,
"Oh! ho! my workers brave,
Delve if you die the death, for I
Must surely trenches have!"
Your muscle and bone
Are mine alone—
I use them at my will—
And what care I

How fast they die,
If they my coffers fill?"

"Ye are all the slaves of my potent will,
As well as your babes and wives,
And I would not nourish your worth and skill,
Not even to save your lives!
Ye shall fetch, and carry, and dig, and hew,
Beneath the broiling sun,
Or ye shall starve—now which will ye do?—
For mercy I have none!"
Your muscle and bone
Are mine alone—
I use them at my will—
And what care I
How fast they die,
If they my coffers fill?"

"I DON'T CARE!"

"I DON'T care!" How many troubles
From these hateful words have sprung?
Far too often falls the sentence
From the lips of old and young.
How it lowers man's true standard!
How it hurries to despair!
Spleen, and spite, and hate are nourish'd
In the baleful "I don't care!"

"I don't care!" Oh! why so common
Should this vile expression be?
Did it ever soothe a sorrow,
Or to flight put misery?
Did it e'er dispel a shadow,
Or bring sunshine anywhere?
Came there ever yet a blessing
With the spiteful "I don't care?"

Pauper, in thy wretched garret,
Did it ever bring thee gold?
Maiden, did it mend the quarrel
Which arose when love grew cold?
Sailor on the boundless ocean,
Would you ever danger dare
On a ship, however worthy,
With the captain "I don't care?"

Heart-crush'd pilgrim on life's highway,
Did it ever bring thee balm?
Toiler roused by man's injustice,
Did it e'er thy spirit calm?
Christian reaching after heaven,
Did it ever lead to prayer?
Parent, did thy child's amendment
Ever follow "I don't care?"

Many a wretch in anguish groaning,
Rack'd and wasted by disease;
Many a thief his crime atoning
In his sin-bought miseries;
Many a low-brow'd, ruthless murd'rer
Doom'd to dangle in the air,
Owe the climax of their follies
To the reckless "I don't care!"

"I don't care!" Oh! let the sentence
Never pass your lips again.
It can never bring you pleasure,
But it may engender pain.
'Mid all Satan's vile inventions,
None more surely can ensnare
Than the worthless, good-for-nothing,
Stupid saying, "I don't care!"

IMPROVE YOUR TIME.

IMPROVE your time—the hours fly,
   And every breath we draw
Brings our swift footsteps nearer
   To Death's eternal shore.
Considering vast eternity,
   Life but a span appears,
Although we may permitted be
   To live a hundred years.

The glorious sun at morning
   Breaks from his rosy bed,
And brightens, till at noonday
   He greets us overhead.
Then to the west descending,
   He hides his brilliant light,
And quickly falls around us
   The sombre pall of night.

So with man's course—all jocund
   Is his fresh morning time,
And strengthening he progresses
   Till he has reach'd his prime;
Then down the hill descending
   Time slowly saps his bloom,
Till aged and exhausted
   He drops into the tomb.

Remember, then, ye thoughtless,
By youth and strength sustain'd,
An hour idly wasted
Can never be regain'd.
The past is gone forever—
The future is unknown—
But the present still is with you,
And that is all your own.

LOOK AHEAD.

YOUTH of bright eye and smooth white brow,
So happy and exultant now,
Viewing the brilliant sky above,
Thy bosom full of faith and love—
Love on, hope on, but still reflect,
The stanchest ship is sometimes wreck'd.
Clouds will obscure the brightest sky,
Fancies most prized take wing and fly—
Weep not the past, for that is dead—
And for the future have no dread,
But look ahead!

Man of mature years, full of care,
With threads of silver in thy hair,
Fretting thyself o'er chances lost,
Thy life-bark sadly tempest-tost—
Deem not that you have lived in vain,
The chances lost may come again.

Up! up! and work! be not cast down—
The sombre clouds that on thee frown
May, ere another day has fled,
Disperse, and sunshine banish dread—
So look ahead!

Decrepit pilgrim, nearly home,
Fear not the change that soon must come—
All living walk toward the grave—
God only takes the life He gave.
Let thy thoughts dwell on things above
And rest content, for "God is Love."
Then youth, strong man, or pilgrim gray,
Remember, while ye toil to-day,
The earth at last must be thy bed,
Strive not for dross—'tis best instead
To look ahead!

THE FIREMAN'S DEATH.

HE slept, and o'er his dauntless brow a shade of sorrow stole,
As though some scene of deep distress was busy with his soul,
When suddenly the dread alarm came ringing shrill and clear,
Cleaving the night air till it struck upon his startled ear.
He bounded up! His practiced eye
Was turn'd upon the lurid sky,
Lit by the flames which, mounting higher,
Soon clothed the night in a robe of fire.

With lightning speed he reach'd the scene—oh! what
a sight was there!
A mother stood amid the flames, and shriek'd in wild
despair!
Her arms around her frighten'd babe were thrown with
frenzied clasp,
As though she fear'd the fire-fiend would tear it from
her grasp.
With helmet turned, through flame and smoke
The gallant fellow fearless broke;
He saved them both, but ah! his life
Was lost in the unequal strife.

Now in sweet Greenwood's peaceful shade the noble
hero sleeps,
And o'er his grave full many a friend in silent sorrow
weeps,
A monument erected there is pointed to with pride
By those with whom he oft has fought the fire, side by
side.
Sweet flowers exhale their fragrant breath
Where now he calmly sleeps in death,
And trees their spreading branches wave
Around his solemn Greenwood grave.

AT SEA UPON LIFE'S OCEAN.

AT sea—we're all at sea upon life's ocean,
And none can boast a never-failing chart—
Sail as we may we'll meet with dread commotion,
And hidden shoals to terrify the heart.

The wisest and most prudent at the helm
May in some fatal hour the wrong course take,
But treacherous seas will surely overwhelm
The mariner who laughs at woe and wreck.

We're all at sea—some favor'd ones, enchanted,
Float peacefully upon the placid tide,
While others with sad doubts and fears are haunted,
And ever on the roughest billows ride.
This difference should not to wonder move us—
'Tis true the law we fail to understand,
But then 'twas wisely framed by One above us
Who holds the mighty ocean in His hand.

We're all at sea! God help that sordid creature
Who grimly gloating o'er his golden hoard,
With avarice making hideous every feature,
Heeds not that dreadful cry, "Man overboard!"
No rest for him afloat; and when disaster
Shall lay him on the ocean broad a wreck,
The gold which he has worship'd as a master
A fearful weight shall hang about his neck.

We're all at sea! and 'tis our common duty
To help a fellow sailor in distress;
Hard gain'd indeed will be that race or booty
To win which leaves on earth one light heart less.
Then let us while we're sailing on life's ocean,
Bless'd by soft gales, beneath kind fortune's star,
Still keep a bright lookout with deep devotion
For those who in their path less favor'd are.

THE HONEST WORKING GIRL.

THE air is chill, the city's pave
Is slippery and wet;
The child of wealth and luxury
Is wrapp'd in slumber yet;
The sleet and snow are rushing by
In many an angry whirl,
While hurries to her daily toil
The honest working girl.

No word have I 'gainst gold to say,
If it be fairly earn'd;
And fairly used by rich men, who
Sweet charity have learned.
The generous merchant may with pride
His banner broad unfurl,
But prouder is the record of
The honest working girl.

Her clothes, though not the finest,
Are the best that she can wear;
Her fingers boast no diamonds,
But her face is very fair;
Her eyes are bright, and when she smiles
She shows her teeth of pearl;
And love dwells in the bosom of
The honest working girl.

With wages scant the ills of life
  She's fated to endure;
And yet she manages to save
  A trifle for the poor.
At any mean or sordid act,
  With scorn her lip will curl,
For noble is the nature of
  The honest working girl.

Then treat her kindly, ye proud ones,
  Who "neither toil nor spin;"
She has to struggle very hard
  Her daily bread to win.
And he—though dress'd in finest cloth—
  Would be a very churl,
Who would not, if appeal'd to, help
  The honest working girl.

God bless the modest, gentle ones
  Who labor day by day!
And God bless those with means to spare,
  Who help them on their way!
Ye who would, in the better land,
  Possess the priceless pearl,
Treat not with scorn, nor cold contempt,
  The honest working girl.

IF YOU CAN'T PRAISE YOUR NEIGHBOR, DON'T NAME HIM AT ALL.

IN our judgment of others, we mortals are prone
To talk of their faults without heeding our own;
And this little rule should be treasured by all:
"If you can't praise your neighbor, don't name him at all."

Men's deeds are compounded of glory and shame,
And surely 'tis sweeter to praise than to blame;
Perfection has never been known since the fall—
"If you can't praise your neighbor, don't name him at all."

Remember, ye cynics, the mote and the beam;
Pause in your fault-finding and ponder the theme;
Who has the least charity, quickest will fall—
"If you can't praise your neighbor, don't name him at all."

If we would endeavor our own faults to mend,
We'd have all the work to which we could attend:
Then let us be open to charity's call—
"If you can't praise your neighbor, don't name him at all."

THE CUBAN VOLUNTEER'S FAREWELL.

COMRADES, I am surely dying,
  Home again I ne'er shall see;
Would that I had died in battle,
  But it was not so to be;
Dying in this loathsome dungeon,
  But my pain will soon be o'er;
How my failing pulse would quicken,
  Could I face the foe once more!
Death I do not fear, my brothers;
  I have met him o'er and o'er;
I would die without a murmur,
  Could I face the foe once more.

When brave, struggling Cuba call'd me,
  I the summons did attend;
Tell my father, if you see him,
  I was faithful to the end.
Give this Bible to my mother;
  Since our tearful last good-by,
It has been my close companion,
  And has taught me how to die.
Death I do not fear, my brothers,
  I have faced him o'er and o'er;
I would die without a murmur,
  Could I meet the foe once more,

Now the shadows gather round me,
　And my life is ebbing fast;
Bear me, comrades, to the window,
　On the sun I'd look my last.
Farewell, now, my heart-sick brothers,
　You will join me by and by;
If you perish here, remember,
　'Tis for freedom you will die.
Death I do not fear, my brothers,
　I have faced him o'er and o'er;
I would die without a murmur,
　Could I meet the foe once more.

Fiends of Spain! Incarnate devils!
　Cuba's sons shall yet be free!
All your cruelty and venom
　Cannot crush out Liberty!
Still survives the holy passion
　That has carried us thus far—
Soon will beam on the horizon
　Cuba's independence star!
Death I do not fear, my brothers,
　I have faced him o'er and o'er;
I would die without a murmur,
　Could I meet the foe once more.

"I CAN'T!" AND "I'LL TRY.

"I CAN'T!" exclaims the truant boy,
  While loitering on the way;
"I can't!" repeats the imbecile,
  Whose locks are streak'd with gray;
"I can't!" It is the common phrase
  Of all inclined to fly
When dangers menace; but the brave
  Would rather say, "I'll try!"

"I can't!" It stultifies the soul
  And palsies all within;
'Tis made the flimsy, weak excuse
  For each besetting sin.
And many an ill that stays by us
  Away would quickly fly,
If we would hold our heads erect
  And firmly say, "I'll try!"

The drunkard says, "I can't!" when he
  Is counselled to abstain;
The sluggard drawls, "I can't!" when told
  By work his bread to gain.
The harden'd thief exclaims, "I can't
  Temptation's door go by!"
But each his fault could master
  If he'd stoutly say, "I'll try!"

"I can't!" Had Fulton thus exclaim'd
When jeer'd at as insane;
Or bold Columbus when his crew
Revolted on the main;
Or brave Galileo, when forced
His theory to disown;
Or Morse, when pinch'd by poverty
And struggling on alone—

Had these brave souls, and many more
Who won the wreath of fame,
Sat down to murmur and lament
When difficulties came,
How many blessings we should miss
Which make us glad to-day,
And what a sombre cloud would on
The hill of science lay.

"I can't!" Oh! drop the hateful phrase,
Ye toilers everywhere;
Be earnest on life's battle-field,
Fail not to do and dare!
Faint not, if stern reverses come,
But fix your faith on high,
And let your noble motto be,
"With God's good help, I'll try!"

LINES WRITTEN IN "OUR CARRIE'S" ALBUM.

LUSTROUS eyes revealing
   Young Love peeping through,
Heart of warmest feeling,
   Nature kind and true;
Lineaments which tell us
   Thou wert born to bless,
Friendship's counsel zealous,
   Gentle Carrie S.

Full of toil and sorrow
   Is this weary life,
Each succeeding morrow
   Brings its care and strife;
But may heavenly power
   Shield *thee* from distress,
Guard thee every hour,
   Trusting Carrie S.

Time may overcome thee,
   Touch thy hair with gray,
Steal thy beauty from thee,
   Take thy strength away;
But thy *soul* will never
   Lose its loveliness;
That will bloom forever,
   Truthful Carrie S.

A PLEA FOR CUBA.

FREEMEN of our great republic,
  Bend to heaven the knee—
Raise your hands and shout the chorus,
  Cuba shall be free!
Spain, vile Spain, with steel and halter,
Hovers over freedom's altar,
Cowards are we if we falter—
  Strike for liberty!

By the graves of our brave sires,
  By their great deeds done,
By sweet freedom's sacred fires
  Lit at Lexington;
By our blood-cemented nation,
By each bondman's aspiration,
By our hopes of dear salvation,
  Do not Cuba shun!

Hark! across the stormy waters
  Comes a piteous cry;
'Tis from Cuba's sons and daughters,
  "Will ye let us die?"
Freemen, up! No longer dally!
Round fair Cuba's standard rally,
From the mountain and the valley—
  Cause her foes to fly!

Shall Spain's stabbers wield the sabre,
  Flush'd with victory?
God forbid! Let's pray and labor!
  Cuba *must* be free!
Clamor for her recognition,
Hurl her tyrants to perdition,
Thus may we fulfil our mission,
  Death to slavery!

TAKE IT EASY!

TAKE it easy, men of muscle!
  Take it easy, men of brain!
You may stumble if you hurry,
  And you nothing then will gain.
Any work that's worth the doing
  Surely is worth doing well;
Rather than by haste destroy it,
  Better stop and breathe a spell.

Take it easy, mirthful maidens!
  Take it easy, girls and boys!
Every pleasure rashly follow'd,
  In the end too surely cloys.
Never haste to grasp the shadow
  When the substance is secure!
Trust me, there is health and safety
  In the motto, "Slow and sure."

Take it easy, slave of passion!
  Hasty words will nothing gain;
While your breast is fill'd with anger,
  All your work will be in vain.
Curb your temper till cool reason
  Has a chance to play its part,
And your task will be the easier,
  And the purer be your heart.

Take it easy, mourning pilgrim!
  Sad at heart and sick at soul,
Why shouldst thou, when heaven is certain,
  Be so swift to reach the goal?
Wait God's time, and thy probation
  On the earth will soon be o'er,
And thou'lt wrestle with temptation
  And heart-sorrow nevermore.

THE KERNEL AND THE NUT.

"He who would eat the kernel must not complain because obliged to crack the nut."—*Old Saying.*

YE who in this changeful life
  Not a ray of joy can see,
Ye who foster care and strife,
  Never from excitement free;
Ye who never seek for peace,
  Hoping it will seek for you,
Daily will your woes increase,
  And you'll find this maxim true:

Earthly joys and joys supernal
From the sluggard mind are shut;
If you wish to taste the kernel,
First you'll have to crack the nut.

Life's stream seldom smoothly flows,
And at times we're forced to mourn;
But who would reject the rose
Even though it has its thorn?
By hard labor we may seize
Pleasure from the lap of pain,
If we idly take our ease,
We shall look for joy in vain.
Earthly joys and joys supernal
From the sluggard mind are shut;
If you wish to taste the kernel,
First you'll have to crack the nut.

Should misfortune weigh you down,
Never yield to dark despair;
Take the cross and win the crown,
Toil for good and laugh at care.
Resolutely strive and plan,
Inactivity is vain,
What would pleasure be to man
If he never tasted pain?
Earthly joys and joys supernal
From the sluggard mind are shut;
If you wish to taste the kernel,
First you'll have to crack the nut.

FOLD UP THE STARRY BANNER.

FOLD up the starry banner,
And put it out of sight—
'Tis laugh'd at by the minions
Of tyranny and spite.
All impotent it flutters
Upon the open sea,
And who shall dare to call it
The banner of the free?

Fold up the starry banner—
Its rainbow glories drape,
In deep humility and woe,
With sombre, solemn crape.
The eagle that watch'd o'er it
Looks down in sad surprise,
And the goddess of sweet freedom
Is weeping where it lies.

Fold up the starry banner,
And hoist the hated rag
Of vile Spain to replace it—
Columbia has no flag.
Her ships are free no longer,
Her gallant tars are slaves,
And all that may be taken
Are doom'd to bloody graves.

Fold up the starry banner,
For sad Columbia weeps,
And Tyranny is gorged with blood,
While Freedom soundly sleeps,
Or if she does not slumber,
She lies subdued and tame,
And all who gloried in her
Are bow'd by grief and shame,

Fold up the starry banner,
Nor let it wave again
Till it can have its proper place
Above the rag of Spain.
Then let it flash its glories
Upon the land and sea,
And those who love it strike one blow
For Cuba's liberty.

THE GODDESS OF LIBERTY.

(WRITTEN ON THE FOURTH OF JULY.)

OH, Goddess of Liberty, radiant and joyous,
Look down on thy favorite nation to-day—
Permit no dissensions nor cares to annoy us—
Drive every shadow of discord away.
Come in thy rare beauty, a laurel-wreath wearing—
Come with the flag of the free in thy hand—
Come in thy eloquent language declaring
Freedom shall never depart from our land.

Speak to us of our dead patriots and sages—
 The foremost of heroes—"the salt of the earth"—
Whose virtue and fame shall descend to the ages
 While freedom's disciples prize honor and worth.
Recall to our minds how the war tocsin sounded
 In "seventy-six," when each sire and son
With shouts of defiance upon the foe bounded
 Till tyranny perish'd and freedom was won.

Oh, beautiful goddess, be thou ever near us,
 To guide and direct us in war or in peace—
To strengthen when faint, when despondent to cheer us—
 When doubting, our faith in our laws to increase.
Then still shall our land, like a beacon-fire burning,
 Invite the oppress'd of all nations to come,
While their desolate heart are for sympathy yearning,
 And find a sure refuge in freedom's bright home.

WORK.

AROUSE, thou sluggard! Leave thy bed so dear,
 Nor longer in thy drowsy chamber lurk;
Walk forth with open eye and listening ear,
 And let kind Nature teach thee how to work.
Turn where you may, each thing in nature's school
 The tale of constant motion will rehearse;
Nothing is idle—labor is the rule
 Which regulates the mighty universe.

By work the ever active honest bee
  With store mellifluous supplies his hive;
The tiny ant by constant industry
  Garners up food to keep himself alive;
Even the plants, whose flowers pass from view
  In winter hoar, are toiling in the earth
For sustenance the dreary season through,
  To give, when Spring-time comes, more sweet buds birth.

By work, the bright stream, singing merrily,
  Is kept pellucid in its onward flow;
Check its glad action—curb its motion free—
  And it will stagnant and offensive grow.
'Tis motion that each planet bright upholds
  Steady and constant in its proper sphere,
As in its course it ever onward rolls—
  'Tis motion that keeps pure the atmosphere.

Then heed the lesson, sluggard! Man was made
  Greater than earth, or air, or stars on high;
For these will surely into nothing fade—
  The soul's immortal and it cannot die.
But by inaction man may torpid grow,
  And drone his life away in useless dreams,
Just as the evils of inaction show
  In stagnant, fetid, death-exhaling streams.

HARD LUCK.

I TOOK my place the other day
  On board a ferry-boat,
And look'd around as is my wont,
  The passengers to note.
Two young mechanics going home
  From work was standing near,
Whose colloquy I listen'd to,
  And will repeat it here.

"O Jack!" said one, "the other day
  I fell against Tom Duff,
And I tell you I pitied him,
  He look'd so awful rough.
His toggery was all in rags,
  No shoes were on his feet,
In fact he look'd as hard a case
  As any on the street.

"I asked about his family.
  His wife, he said, was dead,
And his two little children
  Were suffering for bread.
He'd had no work for nigh a month,
  And gone was all his pluck;
He never could succeed, because
  He'd had such horrid luck."

Jack listen'd to his friend's report,
   And then he heaved a sigh,
And then he said, "I pity Tom; but Bob,
   'Twixt you and I,
This horrid luck we hear about,
   Unless I am mistaken,
Instead of being sent to us
   Is often of our makin'.

"Now, Tom and I were 'prentice boys
   Together, as you know,
And he was very quick to learn,
   While I was very slow.
He always could earn more than me,
   And dress'd like any buck;
But he could never keep a cent,
   He had such awful luck.

"He had no one to work for—
   His wages, every cent,
Were his—while I was forced to pay
   My widow'd mother's rent.
And yet so awful was his luck,
   He never had a dime,
And he has borrow'd stamps from me
   To get beer many a time.

"Both of us married early,
   And both got thrifty wives;
There should have been no difference
   In the current of our lives.

If anything, my expenses
  Were the greatest; for you see
While Tom has but two little ones,
  Kind Heaven has sent me three.

"Tom's wife was young and beautiful,
  But wasn't very strong,
And being obliged to work so hard,
  She couldn't stand it long.
She never ventured out of doors,
  But to her babies stuck,
While Tom sat in some drinking-shop
  A-growling at his luck.

"Now, I've no reason to complain,
  I'm doing very well;
Sometimes indeed when work gives out
  I have an idle spell;
But then I always try to keep
  A stamp or two ahead,
And never yet have had to hear
  My babies cry for bread.

"I'm just as sorry for poor Tom
  As you can be, friend Jack,
And I would rather help him on
  Than try to set him back.
But I have always noticed
  When a fellow guzzles rum
And loafs about and takes his ease,
  Hard luck is sure to come."

THE HORSE.

OF all the lower animals
That humbly tread the earth
To work for careless, thankless man,
The horse has greatest worth.
A very giant in his strength,
And yet withal so mild,
That he will readily obey
An invalid or child.

How patient and how tractable,
How willing he to toil—
A very slave to man, and yet
The monarch of the soil.
The meanest steed is worth regard,
But beautiful to see
Is one of choicest lineage
And perfect symmetry.

No pen can do him justice,
And e'en the limner's art
Will fail a perfect idea
Of the racer to impart.
His form may be depicted,
But the fire in his eye,
The *life* that animates his frame,
These, every art defy.

Height, sixteen hands—his color, black—
An arch'd neck full and strong,
A pair of eyes that shine like stars,
Mane, tail, and foretop, long.
Ears like a fox's, small and sharp,
With nostrils large and thin,
And showing, when expanded wide,
The blood-red tint within.

THE POWER OF STEAM.

OH! be my theme the power of steam—
'Tis greater than sword or pen;
For it furnishes bread, and raiment and bed,
For millions of toiling men.
Day after day it puffs away,
Alike in calm or storm,
And mortals gaze in mute amaze
At what it can perform.

It winnows, it plows, it heads, it blows,
It cuts, it slits, it dresses,
It stamps, it planes, it digs, it drains,
It condenses, collects, and presses.
It forges, it rolls, it melts, it moulds,
It files, it hammers, it rasps,
It punches, it beats, it cooks, it heats,
Releases and tightly grasps.

It propels, it rows, it warps, it tows,
It pulls, it carries, it scatters,

It pushes, it draws, it gouges, it bores,
It polishes, breaks, and batters.
It lowers, it lifts, it grinds, it sifts,
It washes, it smooths, it crushes,
It picks, it hews, it prints the news,
It rivets, it sweeps, it brushes.

It sculls, it screws, it mends, it glues,
It pumps, it irrigates,
It sews, it drills, it levels hills,
Shuts, opens, and elevates.
It extracts, confines, it marks out lines,
It thrashes, it separates,
It mixes, it kneads, it drives, it leads,
It chisels, it excavates.

It stamps, it turns, it hatches, it churns,
It mortises, saws, and shaves,
It bolts, it brings, it lends us wings,
It fights the winds and waves.
It scutches, it cards, advances, retards,
It spins, it twists, it weaves,
It coins, it shears, tear down, uprears,
Discharges and receives.

Then be my theme the power of steam—
'Tis greater than sword or pen;
For it furnishes bread, and raiment and bed,
For millions of toiling men.
Day after day it puffs away,
Alike in calm or storm,
And mortals gaze in mute amaze,
At what it can perform.

WOMAN.

A HEALTH to the lass with the laughing blue eye,
That seems to have borrow'd its hue from the sky—
Where young love is constantly feeding his flame,
And virtue sits blocking the entrance to shame.
Who weeps with the mourning and laughs with the gay,
Who can comfort old age or with infancy play,
Who quarrels with no one, but sticks to her creed—
Here's to her, for she is a woman indeed!

And here's to the girl with the lustrous black eye,
Who one moment may laugh and the next moment sigh;
Whose heart is a casket of joy and of grief,
And the first knows no limit, the last no relief.
Who deeply doth love, but as deeply can hate—
A Christian, and yet a believer in fate—
Who for pity will weep, or in anger will kill—
Here's her health—she is one of the softer sex still!

Here's to the coquette with the optic of gray,
Who will never say yes, but can hardly say nay;
Who falls dead in love with each gay beau she sees,
But can never find one for a long time to please.
Who is anxious to marry, and yet is afraid;
Who lives a young ninny, and dies an old maid;
Though blameful her follies it must be confess'd,
Yet her health—she's a woman as well as the rest.

In fine, here's to woman—the large and the small,
The lean and the fleshy, the short and the tall,
The dark eye, the blue eye, the hazel and gray,
The cheerful and sullen, the grave and the gay.
I care not how faulty their natures may be—
They are women—which fact is sufficient for me;
As mother, friend, sister, maid, widow, or wife,
They are God's best gift to man, the consolers of life.

MEAGHER'S ESCAPE.*

THERE'S a voice in the gale, speeding over the waters,
A song of rejoicing, a burden of glee,
A pean from Erin's brave sons and fair daughters,
"Old Ireland's defender, young Meagher, is free!"
They could not enslave him; for on her broad pinions
The Genius of Liberty day after day
Hover'd over his head, and from tyranny's minions
At length bore the noble-soul'd patriot away.

With honor he shook off the shackles that bound him,
His parole gave up ere he ventured his plan;
And then in broad day, with his enemies round him,
Cried, "Now I defy ye! Take me, if you can!"
But vain their endeavors; his steed like a swallow
Flew over the ground with his rider so brave;
And soon they found out it was useless to follow,
For Meagher was safely afloat on the wave.

* First published under a *nom de plume* in 1852.

Oh! how must the news of the captive's achievement—
    The tidings that he had his liberty won—
Have chased, as the sun does the mist, the bereavement
    Of those who stood round him at Slievenamon!
How eyes must have sparkled and hearts must have
        bounded,
    And hills must have echoed with cheer upon cheer,
From the wild throbbing bosoms that quickly surrounded
    The bonfire that blazed upon Corrigmoclier!

But it is not his country alone that rejoices;
    The republican host of our own cherish'd land
In deep exultation are raising their voices,
    And thronging to grasp the young patriot's hand.
"You are welcome," they cry, "to the land of the
        stranger—
    Thrice welcome beneath our proud eagle's broad
        wing;
Here safely repose thee, exempt from all danger
    Protected forever from tyranny's sting.

RELIGION.

HAIL, blest Religion! safeguard of the free!
    Destroyer of foul vice, mother of purity,
Thou white-robed seraph at whom skeptics rail—
Balm of the bleeding heart, Religion, hail!
Many profess to own thy sacred flame,
And day by day invoke thy blessed name
In gorgeous temples, built with jealous care;
But let's look in and see if thou art there.

See, in yon cushion'd pew, with downcast look,
A man sits poring o'er a well-thumb'd book;
All richly dress'd is he in vestments rare;
And as the holy man pours forth his prayer
His face assumes a penitential air,
Mingled *somewhat,* methinks, with worldly care.
Now his pale countenance betokens pain,
And tears are falling from his eyes like rain!
He reads a memorandum book of loss and gain!
Its contents have convinced him, plain as day,
That some of his dear cash has flown away.
He whispers *her* his loss, and, musing on it,
His wife is grieving for her next new bonnet.

In a darksome corner, almost hid from view,
Sits one who is a villain through and through.
He's dozing now, and now begins to nod,
And, sleeping holds communion with *his* god,
His gilded god: that man his daughter sold—
His only daughter—for a heap of gold.

Now cast your eye on yonder youthful pair,
Who seem Devotion's counterpart—how fair
And pure they look, those lovely girls!
List! their religion's centred in their curls!
"My gracious, Emma! look at Martha's hair!
How illy it's arranged, I declare!"

But turn we round our eyes, and gaze we now
Upon a *Christian,* whose unclouded brow
Speaks the tranquillity that reigns within
His breast. He is not free from sin—

(None are, though some pretend to be,
And elongate their faces piously;
They never smile—not they—they'd sooner cry,
And agonize and groan, and sweat and sigh).
He believes that every creature born of woman
Has passions, and "to step aside is human."
He toiling earns his bread—does all he can
To be what God intended him—a man.

'Twould fill a book to mention every one—
The luckless debtor and the heartless dun;
The widow poor, who scarce her bread can earn,
Rising from prayer to meet the landlord stern;
The beggar, perishing through lack of food,
Doubting the policy of doing good,
And, losing every thought of future weal,
Goes forth from prayer constrain'd almost to steal.

Yes, visit any city church—you'll find
Within its walls all grades of human kind;
But underneath the peasant's humble roof
(From which the rich man sneering stands aloof)
The "peace which passeth understanding" lives—
That priceless peace which *true* Religion gives.
There Nature works, and from the emerald sod
Around the poor man's cottage, up to God
The flowers their incense breathe, as if in prayer;
And every bird that carols in the air,
And every breeze that sweeps the forest wild,
Speaks of Religion, "pure and undefiled."

THE HERO SAILOR.

Lieutenant W. Lewis Herndon, U. S. N., late commander of the U. S. Mail Steamship Central America, was lost at sea September 12th, 1857, by which disaster 326 souls perished, including Captain Herndon, and over $2,000,000 of treasure was lost.

LOOK at his features, ye who read
Man's nature in his face,
And tell me if a single line
Ignoble ye can trace.
Peruse the well-mark'd lineaments
As closely as you can,
And say do they not "give the world
Assurance of a man?"

No giant strength did he possess,
No stalwart, towering form,
Yet with the strength of Hercules
He wrestled with the storm;
'Twas honor nerved the hero's arm
And stirr'd his lion heart,
And taught him how, at duty's call,
With life itself to part.

"There is no hope! It cannot be
That he escaped the wreck!
For he would be the last to leave
The fated vessel's deck!"

Thus spoke, and truly spoke,
The gallant sailor's noble wife;
She knew to keep his honor whole
He'd sacrifice his life.

Weep for his fate, ye maidens,
Wives, and mothers of the land!
On history's page eternally
The glorious truth shall stand,
That in that fearful hour of death
Upon the ocean wild,
Of all on board there was not lost
A woman or a child.

'Twas nobly done, O Herndon!
And thy name shall ever be
In manhood's lexicon a word
Expressing chivalry.
Well may the Old Dominion,
Who gave us Washington,
And many other noble names,
Be proud of such a son.

With placid brow the brave man saw
The helpless ones depart,
And then a heavy load of care
Seem'd lifted from his heart.
He view'd them as they left the ship
Toss'd on the billows wild,
Then from his lips the sentence broke,
"God help *my* wife and child!"

When the ill-fated ship went down,
Of all that luckless band
Alone her brave commander stood,
A rocket in his hand.
To the last gasp he clung to her,
And then, the struggle o'er,
He calmly closed his eyes in death,
And sank to rise no more.

Calm be thy rest, O noble heart!
Upon thy ocean bed;
Than thine there is no worthier name
Among the gallant dead.
Thy fate was mournful, but the world
Shall speak thy virtues rare,
While God-like truth exists, and men
Are brave and women fair.

ELSIE'S DEATH.

"Out of the mouths of babes and sucklings hast Thou ordained strength."—PSALM 8 : 2.

AN infant form lay stark and cold,
In its last sad habit drest,
But the smile on its angel features told
How calm it had sunk to rest.
And tears down its mother's pale cheek roll'd,
As she kiss'd her darling, stark and cold.

A little girl—the dead one's twin—
    Stood gazing on the scene;
She nothing knew of death or sin,
    And wonder'd what could mean
Her mother's lamentations loud
While o'er her darling's corse she bow'd.

"What ails my little sister dear?
    Sweet mamma, tell me, pray.
I've watch'd her lying silent here
    Throughout the livelong day.
She does not seem to feel or hear—
What ails my sister, mamma dear?"

"She's dead, my child; your sister's dead—
    She cannot play again;
Her spirit has forever fled
    From grief, and sin, and pain.
And yet, O God! my heart will break
When my last look at her I take!"

"Mamma, have you not often said
    That when good people die,
They go where no more tears are shed—
    With God, beyond the sky?
I love my sister, mamma dear,
But would not, could I, keep her here.

"For Elsie, I am sure, is there—
    So, mamma, let *us* die;
And to her in that home so fair
    Together let us fly!

I'm very sure, mamma, that *she*
Is watching now for you and me!"

"I thank thee, God!" the mother cried,
"Now I can bear my loss.
Come, kneel, sweet one, with me beside
Your little sister's corse;
Raise up your hands, my precious one,
And pray, 'Thy will, not mine, be done!'"

BIRDS WERE NOT MADE IN VAIN.

A FARMER once,
A youthful dunce,
Stood gazing o'er a field
Of springing corn,
By blackbirds shorn
Of half that it should yield.
Said he, "Bright birds,
Mark ye my words,
Your doom is surely seal'd.

"Ye have had your share,
Of my produce rare;
Ye have ranged my broad fields o'er,
And pick'd and ate
At such a rate
That half my crop or more
Has felt the blight,
Of your greedy bite,
But now your reign is o'er!"

He kept his word;
Each joyous bird
That on the morrow trill'd
His joyous song
The meads along
Was mercilessly kill'd.
"Now," cried the lad,
With visage glad,
"My barn will sure be fill'd!"

Time sped along,
The blackbird's song
No more was heard in air;
The farmer stood
In solemn mood,
And features full of care.
His eye roam'd o'er
The fields, but saw
No vegetation there.

On each green leaf
A reptile thief,
Erst the blithe blackbird's prey,
A full meal had
The farmer lad
Had sent their scourge away,
And the poor wight,
Possess'd not quite
The blackbird's power to slay.

He view'd the scene
With thoughtful mien,

His heart was touch'd with pain.
"O bright wing'd birds!"
He cried, "that words
Would bring ye back again!
For now, in sooth,
I feel the truth,
Birds were not made in vain!"

HE DID NOT READ THE NEWS.

ONE summer's morn to Gotham came
A weary wight, John Smith by name,
Who travell'd hither from the west
The profit of fair trade to test.
His form was bony, lank, and tall,
His clothes were poor, his means were small.
A man he was of narrow views
Who did not care to read the news.

John entertain'd, 'twixt you and me,
Queer notions of economy.
At home he drank, and chew'd—would go
To see the travelling circus show—
Would puff his cash away in vapor,
But couldn't afford to take a paper.
Of fresh events he held no views.
Because he didn't read the news.

Scarce had he got the city in,
Ere his misfortunes did begin;

He sold his cattle, got the cash,
And then resolved to cut a dash.
He started off without delay,
And, whistling, saunter'd down Broadway,
To take an independent cruise—
He didn't care to read the news.

"Say Johnny!" cried a voice, "look here!"
John turn'd and saw a stranger near.
"Why, don't you know me, Cousin John?"
The man—a well-dressed youth—went on,
"Why, I knew you at once, right well!
Come, go with me to my hotel!"
John went—he couldn't see the *ruse*—
Oh! if he had but read the news!

No one will doubt us when we say
John's *cousin* was enrich'd that day,
While hapless John, of sense bereft,
Had only half his money left.
"Gosh!" cried the dupe, with rage and grief,
"A fellow dress'd like that a thief!
I swan! 'twould give a saint the blues!
Oh! don't I wish I'd read the news!"

Deploring his unhappy fate,
He to a drinking shop went straight
His sorrows in a glass to drown;
And when he'd gulp'd the liquor down,
At once his brain began to spin,
For what he swallow'd drugg'd had been,
And soon his senses John did lose.
Poor dupe! He hadn't read the news.

Then many a low-brow'd villain came,
Considering John Smith fair game.
They pluck'd him bare, and not a cent
Had he when to the Tombs he went.
"Judge!" cried the victim, "Judge! look here!
I've lost five hundred dollars clear!
I hope your aid you won't refuse."
"John," said the justice, "read the news!"

A sharp-eyed newsboy standing near
Cried, "Johnny, walk off on your ear!
Don't grumble 'cause you've lost your pelf,
For now you know how 'tis yourself!
You're fortunate, my old galoot,
That some one didn't bust your snoot!
I guess you're one o' them foo-foos
Who never want to read the news!

"If these cops wasn't standin' by,
I'd go to work and break your eye!
I'd like to paste yer in the ear!
I'd like to poultice yer! D'yer hear?
I'd like to take and warm yer jaw
I would, if 'twasn't for the law!
I'm down on these 'ere country Jews,
Too mean to spend a cent for news!"

With heavy heart John left the court,
And quickly he his village sought,
Where safe at last, his friends flock'd round
To learn what fortune he had found.
John eyed them o'er and o'er again
Then, with a visage full of pain,

He said, "Friends, if there's one here who's
A goin' to travel, *read the news!*

"I never have myself, but now
I'll make a solemn, earnest vow
To go, ere speeds another day,
And a full year's subscription pay.
I'll read the paper, every line,
If it takes from six o'clock till nine;
For b'lieve me, friends, a mere recluse
Is he who never reads the news."

WILL YOU LOVE ME THE SAME?

YOU say that you love me, and I will believe thee—
'Tis too late to doubt thee or part from thee now—
Nor have I a thought that you'll ever deceive me
While beauty and freshness are stamp'd on my brow;
But, oh, when that beauty and freshness have faded,
And envious age mars my face and my frame,
And the silver locks come which cannot be evaded—
Oh, in that sad time, will you love me the same?

'Tis sweet, in the spring-time of youthful emotion,
When swift as a racer our wild pulses play,
To drink in the words of a lover's devotion,
Without ever thinking that youth must decay.
I doubt not you'll cling to and cherish me, dearest,
While full is love's fountain and bright is his flame,
But will your love stay with a fervor sincerest
When the romance is gone? Will you love me the same?

OH, KEEP TRUE TO ME!

OH, thou adored, with wondrous beauty beaming!
No limner e'er could copy thy sweet face!
And ne'er did sculptor in his wildest dreaming
Catch e'en a semblance of thy form of grace!
The very air that lifts thy golden tresses
Is odor-laden, having toy'd with thee,
And I am wild with joy at thy caresses;
But time kills beauty—*oh, keep true to me!*

Thy mind is richly stored—bright gems of learning
Fall in a shower from thy ready tongue;
No abstruse study balks thy keen discerning;
Thou art an oracle thy friends among;
Thine eloquence takes captive every hearer,
And moves the dullest soul to ecstasy;
But there's a quality than language dearer—
For words are vapor—*oh, keep true to me!*

Thou holdest in society a proud position—
Thy rank is high, and rich is thy estate—
Broad acres are thine own, and thy condition
Is envied by the greatest of the great.
I cannot choose but laud thy emulation,
And I am very proud thy choice to be;
But beauty, talent, riches, rank and station—
All these may perish—*oh, keep true to me!*

A CHRISTMAS NIGHT VISION.

'TWAS Christmas Eve—and Harry Hall,
His wife and children three,
Sat in their wretched little room
In abject misery.
They had no fire, they had no food,
Their frames were almost bare,
And the sad group a picture form'd
Of hopeless, blank despair.

"I wish old Santa Claus would come, mamma,"
Cried little Sue,
"For I am cold as I can be
And very hungry too.
But then you know he will not come
Till we are all in bed,
So let us go, and then perhaps
He'll bring us clothes and bread."

And so the wretched family
Went to their bed of straw,
And Harry Hall, at dead of night,
A blessed vision saw—
A vision of old Santa Claus
Replenishing the fire,
And loaded down with everything
His sad heart could desire.

Upon his shoulders, broad and strong,
Large packages he bore,
Containing wholesome bread and clothes—
And near him, on the floor,
A sack of coals was open'd wide,
From which, with looks elate,
He fill'd, while pulling at his pipe,
A scuttle near the grate.

It was a blissful, blessed dream
That Harry Hall slept through,
And best of all, when morning broke,
He found the vision true.
A brother, who had years before
The ocean gone across,
Had just return'd in time to be
Poor Harry's Santa Claus.

And now a word to Santa Claus,
The generous and true,
And then I'll have accomplish'd
The end I had in view.
Remember in these panic times
That many girls and boys
Want bread, and meat, and clothes, and fire,
As well as sweets and toys.

So don't forget, old Santa Claus,
The picture drawn above;
And when you start on Christmas Eve
Upon your work of love,

If you would bring a throb of joy
   To many an aching heart,
Put food, and clothes, and coals, as well
   As candies, in your cart.

TO THE BABY.

CROW, kick, and stretch, baby!
   Though crowing be a *fowl* offense,
It cannot touch thy innocence:
And though thy tiny, unskill'd ear,
Like that of noisy chanticleer,
No knowledge hath of time or tune
At present, it will alter soon,
And you may try a higher strain;
But till such time I say again,
   Crow, kick, and stretch, baby!

   Crow, kick, and stretch, baby!
Though kicking may not be genteel
Except in polka, jig, or reel,
Thou canst not yet essay to dance
The latest hop brought o'er from France;
And so thy feet should privileged be
To kick the air right merrily.
Till thou hast learn'd the power of song,
And thy young limbs are lithe and strong,
   Crow, kick, and stretch, baby!

Crow, kick, and stretch, baby!
Stretching was e'er the wisest plan
For helpless babe or grown-up man.
Man, shrinking 'neath the frown of care,
Should stretch to keep his head in air,
And babe, if he would thrive and grow,
Should stretch himself from top to toe.
Then till the difference 'twixt the two
You learn, I'll tell thee what to do—
Crow, kick, and stretch, baby!

CUBA.

FIGHTING 'gainst tyranny, hatred, and spite—
Fighting for liberty—fighting for right—
Fighting 'gainst despots and bloodthirsty knaves—
Fighting to ransom a legion of slaves.
Fighting 'gainst odds, independence to gain,
Nerved by the ghosts of the innocents slain—
Fighting to win—oh, fidelity rare!—
Year after year, with no sign of despair.

Oh, why does Columbia, insulted by Spain,
Outraged and derided, again and again,
Look on while her banner is trailed in the dust
By the bloodthirsty monsters of rapine and lust?
Oh, where is the spirit that guided our sires,
And the vestals that watch'd over liberty's fires?
The fires have gone out and the spirit has fled,
And Freedom, sweet goddess, lies prostrate and dead!

How long shall we treat with these butchers of Spain?
How long shall the brave Cubans struggle in vain?
How long shall the weak be cut down by the strong,
And their blood cry for vengeance? Just Heaven! How
long?
Oh, had we a Jackson to lead us again,
How soon would he scatter these vermin of Spain!
Yea, "by the Eternal!" their scourge he would be,
Till tyranny perish'd and Cuba was free.

What settlement have we effected with Spain?
They will give back our ship—can they give back our
slain?
They will try the vile butchers who slaughter'd her crew,
But will they garrote them as they ought to do?
No! Burriel boldly defies Castelar,
As he views the Republic's fast-paling star;
And what he has done he will do o'er again
In spite of all orders from paralyzed Spain.

The protocol's fix'd up in excellent shape,
And now we must live for awhile on red tape.
We'll swallow the dose that the nations may see,
How humble, and pliant, and meek we can be.
And when we have waited till Burriel is gorged
With the blood of more victims, and more chains are
forged,
Of the protocol awkward no further we'll speak,
But drop the whole subject and "swallow the leek."

RAT, THE NEWSBOY.

ON A LATE FRIGHTFUL ACCIDENT.

MY name is Jimmy Connors, which they calls me Rat, for short—
I'm fourteen, weigh a hundred pounds, likewise I'm fond of sport.
I'm a newsboy, and a bootblack, and I carry bundles too—
In fact, I tackle any job that I am fit to do.

You ask about the accident that happen'd at the ferry—
I'd rather talk of something else—it makes me feel bad—very.
I can't drive it from my mind, sir, oh! it was a fearful sight.
I'm thinking of it all day long and dream of it at night.

But as you seem to wish it, I'll tackle it once more,
And tell you, near as possible, exactly what I saw.
'Twas on Sunday, as you know, sir, and nearly one o'clock,
And I was with my brother, a-fishin' on the dock.

We hadn't been a-sittin' on the stone pier very long,
When suddintly we heard the sound of steam a-blowin' strong.

And then there came a rumblin' noise, and then a
crash—a snorter!
And then my brother lost his seat and tumbled in the
water.

I was dizzy for a minnit, so suddint was the shock,
And then I stirr'd myself to help my brother on the
dock.
I roar'd to see him crawlin' out, and then I fell to
chaffin';
But in a minnit more, you bet, I didn't feel like laffin'.

Quicker'n I can tell it, there came a rush o' steam,
But 'bove the noise it made I heard a hundred people
scream;
My hair riz up, my blood ran cold, so orful did it sound,
And then a crowd of drownin' folks were strugglin' all
around!

It wasn't long before I saw two babies by me float,
And then, like winkin', I threw off my shoes, and vest,
and coat,
And plungin' in, I swam to 'em, and brought 'em safe
ashore;
And then I hurried back agin, to try and save some
more.

I came near blubberin', you bet, but 'twas no time for
cryin'
When men and women, boys and girls, were all around
us dyin';

And so I labor'd with a will till I was tired out,
And then I stopp'd awhile to rest myself and then to
look about.

And such a sight I hope, sir, I shall never see again!
Some dead and others dying—some ravin' mad with
pain!
The air was full of screams, and oaths, and prayers,
and sighs, and groans—
Some had no arms nor legs—some had the flesh torn
from their bones!

I rested but a minnit when I went to work again,
For lookin' at such sights, you bet, went rather 'gainst
the grain.
I'm nothin' but a boy, sir, but I did the best I could;
If I had been a man, I think I might ha' did some
good.*

And now, in few words as I could I've told you all I
saw.
And so, not wishin' to offend, I think I'll chin no more;
I'm onto bissiness now, you see, for it is after nine—
Your boots is very dirty, sir—say, won't you take a shine?

* It is estimated that "Rat" saved at least ten persons.

YOU SPEAK AN UNTRUTH.

YOU speak an untruth when you say that you love me—
That I am the nearest and dearest of all—
That in your esteem there is no one above me—
That no other beauty your heart can enthrall.
You tell me all this while your pulses are leaping
With the maddening warmth of a passion that kills,
While conscience is silent and reason is sleeping,
And the subtle tongue speaks what impurity wills.

You tell me you love me with deepest devotion,
And in the next moment your heart you disclose,
Awakening within me a painful emotion
By uttering what you should blush to propose.
If you had a rich jewel, say, would you impair it
By purposely soiling its beauty so bright?
Nay, would it not rather delight you to wear it
With not a ray lost from its dazzling light?

And am I worth less than a glittering jewel,
That idly you'd bring a reproach to my name,
And in your blind passion, remorseless and cruel,
Destroy my heart's quiet and tarnish my fame?
I've lov'd, and still love thee—how hard the confession!—
All selfish, and heartless, and false as thou art—
But leave me! I cannot forgive thy transgression—
'Twill live in my brain and is sear'd on my heart!

Oh, man of the world! oh, proud minion of fashion!
  Among the gay bowers of pleasure you rove,
And sacrifice oft on the altar of passion
  The hearts that, untouch'd, would be sacred to love.
Oh, fond, feeble woman, when temptation meets you,
  Let prudence and purity sound the alarm—
Remember this fact, when a libertine greets you;
  No man *loves* the woman he's willing to harm.

WHY NOT FORGIVE HIM?

WHY not forgive your brother
  If he comes to you in sorrow?
Why not your anger smother
  Ere the dawning of to-morrow?
You say he has reviled you
  Your dearest friends among—
But has error ne'er beguiled you?
  Have you ne'er committed wrong?
          Why not forgive him?

He is penitent and humble—
  He is weak and in your power—
Who is not apt to stumble
  When passion rules the hour?
He wrong'd you in his blindness—
  Now act the Christian's part,
And pour the balm of kindness
  On his sad, repentant heart.
          Why not forgive him?

Can you look for sweet contentment,
 Or can love your bosom fill,
While you cherish fierce resentment
 For the one who treats you ill?
No! Spite of proud position—
 Of place, or power, or pelf,
Unblest is your condition
 Till you triumph o'er yourself.
  Why not forgive him?

With grief his heart is riven—
 And can you with reason pray
That your sins may be forgiven,
 When from him you turn away?
Vaunt not your pure condition,
 Nor back forgiveness keep—
Think of God's admonition
 "As ye sow so shall ye reap!"
  Why not forgive him?

MAGIC.

THE magic, oh, the magic, in a pair of brilliant eyes!
 Now twinkling with merriment—now looking very wise—
Now glorious with the love-light that hope and joy impart—
Now beaming with a passion that electrifies the heart!

The magic, oh, the magic, in a pair of pouting lips!
Now dewy with the balmy breath which love ecstatic sips,
Now sweetly tantalizing by a gesture grave and coy—
Now wreathed in smiles bewitching and welling o'er with joy!

The magic, oh, the magic, in a sweet voice, soft and low—
Now thrilling us with rapture—now touching us with woe—
Now uttering in softest tones heart-satisfying words—
Now warbling notes that far excel the melody of birds.

The magic, oh, the magic in a loyal, loving soul!
What shall its heaven-born, beatific qualities control?
'Neath its mysterious influence we sorrow or rejoice,
It speaks in form and motion, and in eyes and lips and voice.

MY FATE.

I MET my fate long years ago—
  A being fair as Venus—
But she was wed and chaste as snow,
  And no word pass'd between us.
I felt the pain of love's keen dart,
  And yet no thought I hinted,
But on my palpitating heart
  Her image was imprinted.

Her face and figure wove a spell
  While her bright eyes were beaming,
Which, to my thinking, would excel
  A sculptor's wildest dreaming.
I could not rest, I loved her so!
  But still I gave no token,
For she was wed and chaste as snow,
  And not a word was spoken.

And still I dared her gaze to meet,
  And still I linger'd near her,
For oh, it was so tempting sweet
  To look at and to hear her!
Her voice so musical and low,
  My bosom sadly flutter'd,
But she was wed and chaste as snow,
  And not a word was utter'd.

We parted and we met again—
  She was a wife no longer—
Time had not cancell'd my sweet pain
  But only made it stronger;
And freely then I let her know
  How she my bosom haunted,
For she was free and chaste as snow,
  And I spoke out undaunted.

And now, oh, joy! we mated are—
  Her eyes are on me beaming—
They 'mind me of the lucky star
  That rose on my love-dreaming.
Come joy, come sorrow, weal or woe,
  No ill our hearts can sever,
For she is wed and chaste as snow,
  And she is mine forever.

BURRIEL, THE BUTCHER.

BLOODTHIRSTY Burriel, cursed be thy house!
Thou type of the tiger, the snake and the mouse!
The tiger, who in bloody diet delights—
The venomous snake, who without warning bites—
The cowardly mouse, who will start at a sound—
Their qualities make up thy loathsome compound.

Thou pitiless monster! thou vile hound of Spain!
Whose horrid fangs reek with the blood of the slain,
Thou revellest now in thy gore-spatter'd lair,
But thy cruel heart will be smote by despair
When justice o'ertakes thee—and traced on the wall
You see the handwriting that heralds thy fall.

And history shall record when thou art no more
The deeds of the vulture, who revelled in gore,
And thy name shall be utter'd in ev'ry pure home
With deep detestation for ages to come,
And all will agree that our sin-burden'd earth
Ne'er gave such a venomous man-monster birth.

And thy soul—what of that? when to torture eternal
It crosses the Styx to the regions infernal,
Old Charon will shudder with dread lest his bark
Should sink with a burden so heavy and dark;
And when thou fast anchor'd in Tophet shalt be,
Grim Satan will tremble to look upon thee.

FAREWELL.

FAREWELL! my dream of love is o'er—
    The magic spell is ended—
I'll never gaze upon thee more,
    Thou vision rare and splendid!
There is no power in thine eyes
    To thrill or to enslave me,
Since I have pierced thy weak disguise,
    And now my pride must save me.

Farewell! I would not wed thee now
    To gain uncounted treasures—
I leave with thee thy broken vow,
    The bright world and its pleasures.
Live thou amid the proud and gay,
    Extoll'd caress'd, diverted,
To wake from folly's dream some day,
    By all the world deserted.

Farewell! and when the fatal blow,
    Which well I know awaits thee,
Pierces thy heart with keenest woe,
    And crushes and prostrates thee,
Then think of him whose heart you cleft—
    Unthinking and unsparing—
Of peace, of hope, of joy bereft,
    And drove him forth despairing.

IN TIME.

EVERY wrong shall righted be,
In Time.
Vice shall surely blighted be,
In time.
Vice is reckless and defiant—
Virtue strong and self-reliant—
Sin will surely wreck her client,
In time.

Every trial must be ended,
In time.
Every ill will be amended,
In time.
Guilt may hide, but not securely—
Her disguise deceives but poorly—
Stern-brow'd justice finds her surely.
In time.

Punishment o'ertakes transgression,
In time.
Fate compels a full confession,
In time.
None can safely sin forever—
Conscience leaves the bosom never.
It will crush guilt's best endeavor,
In time.

Sad soul, patience! doubt will vanish,
In time—
Truth's pure light will darkness banish,
In time.
Wait for peace till fate reveals it—
It is near, but Heaven conceals it—
Just the law, till Heaven repeals it,
In time.

SWEET MEMORIES.

WHEN winter hurls her bitter sleet
Across the unprotected moor,
The traveller with hasty feet
Speeds on toward his cabin door;
But though the sharp-fang'd nipping air
May crust his beard with icy rime,
It cannot from his memory tear
The sweet delights of summer-time.

So every memory borne of joy
Will live as long as life shall last;
No changes can the charm destroy—
'Tis proof 'gainst every arrow cast,
A backward view recalls the hours
That once our youthful pulses thrill'd,
As aromatic summer flowers
Live in the scents from them distill'd.

The memory of a childhood pass'd
  Beneath a gentle mother's sway,
With love's sweet mantle o'er it cast,
  Can never wholly pass away.
Whatever adult fate we earn,
  Whate'er the censure or the praise—
Still will the fond heart sometimes turn
  Back to those careless, happy days.

Then let us, as we journey on,
  Endeavor some sad heart to cheer—
'Twill be an act to think upon
  When ending our probation here—
A joy to know that after death
  Has set the restless spirit free,
There still lives in our mortal breath
  Some fondly cherish'd memory.

THE END.

www.ingramcontent.com/pod-product-compliance
Lightning Source LLC
LaVergne TN
LVHW010230110826
845151LV00004B/1244
* 9 7 8 1 4 2 5 5 2 5 9 0 3 *